Your first layer

DISCOVER THE 3D PRINT

by

Michael Hau

Book Cover by Midjourney AI and Michael

Illustrations and Pictures by Michael Hau

2nd Edition Dec 2024

ISBN 9798344453606

Foreword

Welcome to the captivating realm of 3D printing, a space where the lines between science fiction and reality are delightfully blurred. Whether you're a passionate beginner just uncovering the boundless potential of 3D printing or a seasoned professional seeking fresh avenues to expand your expertise, this book can be your ticket to a journey of enhanced understanding and skills in 3D printing. But remember, this book is not just a guide, it's a fan project-a labor of love from one enthusiast to another.

This book is a project of the heart - by a 3D printing enthusiast for other enthusiasts. I would be delighted to receive your feedback on Amazon, and of course, I hope you find it enjoyable! I am not a professional author, but I share my experiences from the last few years in 3D printing. My first printer was a Creality Ender - a real highlight back then, even if it seems a bit old-fashioned compared to today. However, I learnt an incredible amount with this simple machine, especially regarding troubleshooting. I want to share these experiences with you in this book. You have the choice: you can buy a 3D printer that works perfectly straight out of the box - or you can take on the challenge. Opt for a model you must assemble, calibrate and optimise yourself. It will sometimes go smoothly on the first print, but that's the appeal. Solving these small challenges will give you valuable experience that will help you long-term.

You have a choice: either you take the easy route and buy a printer that is delivered almost ready to use and works straight away with minimal effort. Or you can go one step further and take on the challenge. You choose a printer that you must assemble, calibrate and gradually improve yourself - which may not be perfect the first time you print it. But this is precisely where the opportunity lies: you immerse yourself in the material, learn the technology from the ground up and are ideally equipped for future challenges.

3D printing technology, particularly Fused Deposition Modelling (FDM),

has developed rapidly in recent years. What once began as a prototyping tool in industry and research has evolved into a ubiquitous technology that now graces the living rooms of hobbyists worldwide. From helpful household items to artistic sculptures and customised spare parts, 3D printing has fundamentally changed the way we approach making objects.

This book celebrates the creative freedom and technical sophistication made possible by 3D printing. It starts with an introduction to the basics: What is FDM printing, and how does it work? Which printer is best for you? We will guide you step by step through the entire process - from the initial material selection to the finished print. We delve deep into the subject matter and provide details to inspire beginners and challenge professionals.

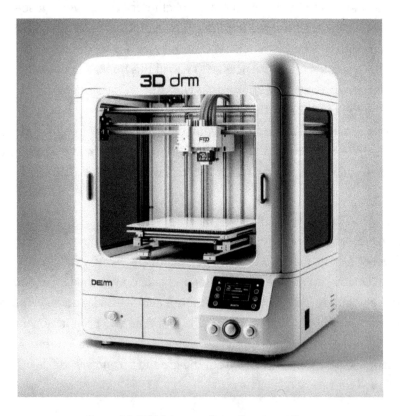

Figure 1 A 3D Printer seen from AI – almost there

In addition to technical explanations and practical tips, some chapters contain a small, not-too-hidden Easter egg from a sci-fi series. These passages are not just for entertainment but also symbolise the bridge between the fiction of days gone by and today's technology.

We aim to give you the tools you need for 3D printing and sensitise you to the ecological aspects of this technology. From handling different filaments to the latest developments in printer software, we cover everything you need to succeed in this exciting field.

Whether you dream of making your creations or want to reprint the work of others, this book will be your faithful companion. Let yourself be enchanted by the world of 3D printing and discover how you can turn your wildest dreams into reality.

Have fun with it!

For my darling: Thank you for reawakening my creativity. ILY

Content

Welcome to the world of 3D printing

The magic of 3D printing

In a world where creativity and technological innovation go hand in hand, 3D printing is at the forefront of a revolution. This technology, once considered a futuristic concept, is now a tangible reality that allows us to transform ideas into physical objects. 3D printing pushes the boundaries of what is possible and opens new horizons for designers, engineers, artists, and hobbyists worldwide. Imagine a process where complex, customised objects can be created layer by layer from nothing, whether at home or in the office. This is the world of 3D printing - a place where the only limitation is your imagination.

A brief history of 3D printing

The journey of 3D printing began in the 1980s when Chuck Hull, considered the father of 3D printing, conducted the first successful experiment with the technology. Hull's invention, stereolithography (SLA), laid the foundation for the development of fused deposition modelling (FDM) technology, which is now one of the most widely used methods of 3D printing. Over the years, 3D printing has evolved from an expensive, complex technology primarily used in industry to an affordable, user-friendly tool for the mass market. This evolution has put 3D printing in the hands of millions of enthusiasts and professionals worldwide who now have the power to bring their most creative ideas to life.

The basics of the FDM printing process

The FDM printing process begins with a digital design created in specialised software. This design is then broken down into a series of thin, horizontal layers that the 3D printer builds up one by one. The desired three-dimensional object is finally created by heating plastic filaments to the melting point and precisely applying these molten materials layer by layer. This method allows you to work with various materials, including PLA, ABS and PETG, making FDM printing versatile. The key to successful printing is precisely controlling temperature, movement and layer thickness to achieve the printed object's best possible quality and strength.

The 3D printer market today

As you read this paragraph, the book is already outdated. Nothing is changing as fast as the 3D printer market. But let's try anyway. In recent years, the popularity of 3D printing has led to rapid growth in the market for Consumer FDM printers. Companies such as Elegoo, Prusa Research, Anycubic, and Creality are at the forefront of this development, offering printers that cover a wide range of price and performance requirements. These manufacturers focus on improving the accessibility and ease of use of their devices while providing advanced features for professional users. Choosing the right 3D printer depends on many factors, including the type of projects you want to realise, your budget and the desired print quality. A thorough understanding of the specifications and capabilities of the different models is crucial to making an informed decision that meets your needs.

Added to this is the growing desire for multi-colour 3D printing. It is hardly surprising that a manufacturer presents a new multi-colour printer in a press release almost every week. The colourful world of 3D printing is becoming increasingly diverse—a reason to rejoice!

The infinite possibilities of 3D printing

3D printing opens up a universe of possibilities, from practical applications such as manufacturing spare parts and tools to creative projects such as artwork and personalised gifts. The technology has also enabled significant advances in medicine, where it is used to produce prostheses, orthopaedic implants, and even 3D printing of tissues and organs in biomedical research. 3D printing encourages a culture of innovation and experimentation by allowing individuals and companies to rapidly prototype and realise ideas without the limitations of traditional manufacturing methods.

In a famous space series that explores the frontiers of space where no one has gone before, machines that can mould and transform matter will play a central role. These fascinating contraptions, capable of creating almost anything from anything, from essential foodstuffs to the most complicated technological gadgets, reflect the visionary mind that often anticipates future possibilities. Now that we live in an era where machines turn digital blueprints into tangible realities, fiction seems less distant than ever.

Summary and outlook

This chapter has given you an insight into the fascinating world of 3D printing. We have explored the origins of this revolutionary technology, explained the basic principles of the FDM printing process and demonstrated the many possibilities of 3D printing. In the rest of this book, we will dive deeper into the technical, creative and practical aspects of 3D printing. Prepare to gain the skills and knowledge to realise your own 3D printing projects and become part of this exciting revolution.

The core components of a 3D printer

The key to successful 3D printing lies in understanding the main components of a 3D printer. These components work together in harmony to create tangible objects from digital designs. Each component has a specific role, and its optimal function is crucial to the end result. In this chapter, we look at the essential components of a 3D printer, explain their function, point out possible sources of error in the event of incorrect maintenance or adjustment and discuss the significant influence on the end result.

Figure 2 Opened direct extruder with filament

Extruder

The extruder is the centrepiece of every 3D printer, transporting the filament to the nozzle. It consists of a motor that pushes the filament through a narrow path into the hot nozzle, which is melted and finally applied to the print bed. Poor maintenance or incorrect adjustment of the extruder, such as excessive tension on the filament or a blockage, can lead to an uneven filament flow, affecting print quality.

- A Bowden extruders connect the nozzle and filament drive through a long tube, which makes the print head lighter and enables fast movements. However, it is more wobbly to print—compare it to pushing up a cooked noodle in a straw. Printing with TPU will be difficult.

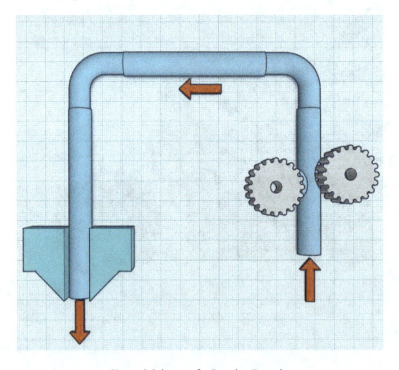

Figure 3 Scheme of a Bowden Extruder

-   In a direct extruder, the gear is located directly above the nozzle, reacts immediately to filament movements and is ideal for flexible materials. Much more precise when retracting, helping to avoid stringing

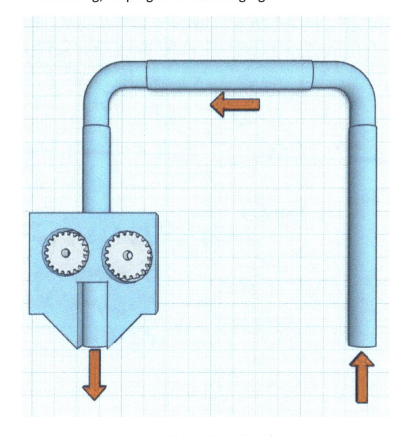

Figure 4 Scheme Direct Extruder

If you suddenly realize during printing that no more filament is being fed while the extruder is clicking frantically, it may be that the gears can no longer feed the filament. This may be because the temperature of the nozzle is too low or the filament has been abraded with many retractions over a short distance and the gears can no longer grip it.

Nozzle

The nozzle is the starting point at which the molten filament is applied to the print bed. Its size influences the level of detail and the layer thickness of the print. A clogged nozzle can lead to incomplete prints or damage to the extruder. Regular cleaning and, if necessary, replacement are essential for consistent print quality. However, each printer has its own nozzle. For example, the nozzle of the 0815 model may not fit the 0816 model and vice versa. The same applies to the PTFE tubes feeding the filament from the extruder into the hothead.

Figure 5 Various nozzles and PTFE tubes

Hotend

As the name suggests, the hotend is the hot end of the print head. The filament is pushed through the extruder, usually through a PTFE tube, into the hot end. Similar to the nozzle, the hotend of the 0815 model is not identical to the hotend of the 0816 model, as seen in the following image. It is, therefore, advisable to wait to buy the hotend and nozzle in stock until you know which printer you have.

Figure 6 Hotends from two printer models.

Red Cable connects to the Heatcartridge which heats the Heat block and so the Nozzle, the white Cable connects to the Thermistor which controls the proper heating (see next page).

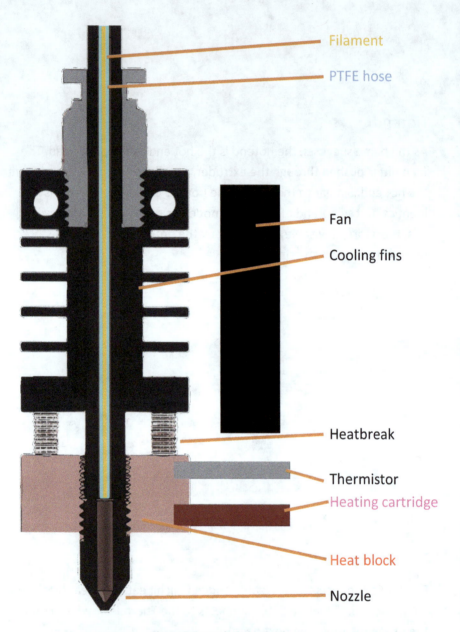

- Filament
- PTFE hose
- Fan
- Cooling fins
- Heatbreak
- Thermistor
- Heating cartridge
- Heat block
- Nozzle

Figure 7 Example Print Head

Print bed

The print bed is the platform on which the 3D object is built. The adhesion of the first layer to the print bed is crucial for the success of the entire print. A poorly calibrated or dirty print bed can lead to incorrect prints. Heated print beds help to minimise deformation of the material and improve adhesion. There are different types of print beds. The most common are printing beds made of glass or metal. Today, PEI beds are usually installed or can be retrofitted cheaply.

Depending on the printer model, the print bed is one of your biggest challenges. Most consumer 3D printers are produced in large quantities in Asia, where attention is only sometimes paid to the last millimetre. It is, therefore, all the more important that you take the time to calibrate your print bed as precisely as possible. If possible, you should re-level your printer before each printing process; for a print that can take up to 10 hours, 5 minutes for levelling is time well spent. Tools like Klipper add-ons, such as KAMP, can further speed up this process.

Figure 8 PEI Printbed

If the adhesion of a PEI print bed could be better, this is usually due to a misaligned Z-offset. Sometimes, and if your Z-Offset is set correctly, the adhesion of a print bed can be increased with a glue stick. The glue stick residue can be washed off later with lukewarm water and soap. However, as modern soaps also contain skin-caring additives such as creams, the PEI plate should be wiped with pure alcohol and a lint-free cloth. This will optimise adhesion.

If the Z offset is set too low, the nozzle will draw unsightly tracks in its print bed, which can also deform it.

Figure 9 Aliens? No, here, a nozzle has dug deep into the PEI plate

! Tip: However, it is always crucial that you only operate your printer with such a plate. Your printer uses a magnetic contact to level the print head or homing (centring). This magnetic contact needs the metallic PEI plate as a counterpole. If this plate is not on the printer while the print head is levelling, it will drive into the material underneath without stopping and probably wreck itself.

PEI, PEO ?

Spring plates for 3D printing beds use different coatings and materials, usually labelled with abbreviations. These designations describe either the material, the surface finish or unique properties of the plate. Here are some of the more common abbreviations you mentioned and their meaning:

1. PEI (polyetherimide): A typical coating applied to spring steel plates. It is known for its adhesion properties and is well-suited for various filaments such as PLA, PETG and ABS.

2. PEO (Plasma Electrolytic Oxidation): This surface treatment is often used on aluminium and other metals to create a rigid, adhesive surface. However, it is less common in 3D printing than PEI.

However, each manufacturer also likes to create its own name to create a unique selling point. Feel free to search for print beds at the Chinese wholesaler and be surprised by the selection. Sometimes, however, the print beds supplied are not the best quality. If you can't get the print to stay on the bed even with the best cleaning and levelling, buy another, higher-quality print bed support.

Gantry

The gantry system refers to the frame structure and mechanical components that enable the extruder and print bed movement in all three axes (X, Y and Z). Accurate alignment of the gantry system is critical, as inaccuracies directly impact print quality. Loosening or wear on the connecting elements can lead to layer shifts and inaccuracies in the print.

Rails

The rails or guide rails are part of the gantry system and enable smooth and precise movement of the extruder and the print bed. Wear or soiling of the rails can cause vibrations or jerking, negatively affecting the printing process's precision. Regular cleaning and lubrication are necessary to maintain the rails' service life and functionality.

Filament sensor

The filament sensor monitors the availability and flow of filament. It can pause or stop printing if the filament runs out or is blocked, reducing material waste and allowing problems to be rectified without having to restart the printing process completely. Without such a sensor, the printer would continue to operate in the event of a filament problem, resulting in faulty or incomplete objects.

Display

The display of a 3D printer enables direct interaction with the device and provides access to settings, print previews and the progress of the printing process. An intuitive and responsive display significantly improves the user experience. Problems with the display can make it difficult to operate and complicate troubleshooting printing issues. Simple and inexpensive entry-level printers usually only have a display with a rotary knob, for example, while higher-priced printers offer a touch display. Klipper printers also provide the advantage of a connection to the home network and a user interface in the web browser.

Each of these components plays a crucial role in the 3D printing process. Careful maintenance, precise settings and an understanding of their functions are essential to achieve the best printing results. As with any complex system, knowing how it works and the potential sources of error is key to minimising problems and maximising the performance of your 3D printer.

Deciphering 3D printing jargon

This chapter guides you through the maze of technical terms that every budding 3D printing enthusiast should know. We dive deep into the subject matter and explain the functions, structure, potential sources of error and the influence of these components and phenomena on the result of your print project.

Layer Shift

Imagine you are building a house of cards, but suddenly, one card shifts and causes the entire structure to shake. Layer shift in 3D printing is similar. The layers shift unexpectedly, resulting in incorrect alignment of the printed objects. Common causes are loose belts, insufficient stepper motor tension, or collisions between the print head and the object. Accurate calibration and maintenance of the printer are crucial to avoid this problem.

Figure 10 Layer Shift

Warping

Warping occurs when the corners of a print object detach from the print bed and curl upwards, similar to how wood warps when exposed to moisture. This warping is caused by uneven material cooling and can be minimised by a heated print bed or an optimised room temperature.

 Tip: Warping can be triggered by direct draughts on the print bed (close the window or heat the room to a comfortable temperature). You can also set the temperature for each slicer differently for the first layer and the following layers. For example, I print the first layer with PLA at 80°C Bed Temperature and all subsequent layers at 60°C)

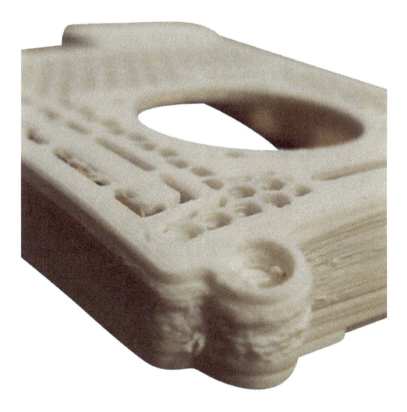

Figure 11 Poor warping

Stringing and oozing

Stringing occurs when thin, cobweb-like threads form between the parts of a 3D print because the molten filament pulls during the movement of the extruder. This can happen either if the extruder does not retract the filament fast enough (settings in the slicer), i.e. pulls it back, if the temperature of the filament is too high (PLA print with PET profile) or if the filament is moist (as in the picture).

 Tip: Fine stringing can be easily removed with a hair dryer or a small gas burner. Oozing refers to excess material escaping from the nozzle when not printing. Both phenomena are often caused by excessively high temperatures or inadequate retraction settings.

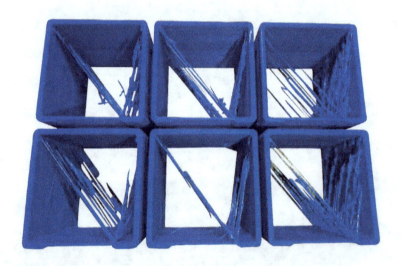

Figure 12 Nice but ugly Stringing

Slicing

Refers to cutting your design into individual slices to prepare it for the printer. See also "Slicing: From model to print."

Blob of Death (or Doom)

It's not always the end of the hot end, but it isn't very pleasant. Sometimes the nozzle is not tightened tightly enough when the printer is assembled at the factory (once again, please check ALL screws when assembling the printer). Under the pressure of the extruder, the filament then looks for the easiest way (good old physics). Nevertheless, the hotend is not lost. Heat the hot end to the printing temperature and carefully remove all filament residues. In this picture, the work could have been done more carefully, and the cable to the thermistor was destroyed. However, thermistors and hotends can be bought new and cheaply online. A Chinese electronics wholesaler usually sells a hotend with a new nozzle in a package for around €15.

Figure 13 Blob of Death with defective thermistor

Figure 14 Blob of Death. On the left is the stepper motor of the extruder

Extrusion

Extrusion is a central process in 3D printing.

Plastic filament is heated in an extruder and pressed through the nozzle. Like toothpaste squeezed out of a tube, the molten filament is applied layer by layer to the print bed to form the 3D model. The precision of the extrusion process is crucial to the quality of the final product; too much material leads to overhangs, and too little to gaps or weak spots. Therefore, carefully calibrating the extruder temperature and filament flow is essential to achieving clean and solid printing results.

Retracting

Retracting, also known as retraction, is an essential term in 3D printing and describes the process by which the extruder retracts the filament. This happens at moments when the print head is moving, but there is no filament to extrude. Retraction prevents oozing or stringing, i.e. the unwanted escape of molten filament, which can lead to threads or lumps on the print object or even prolonged retraction when you want to change the filament and unload the print head.

Precise retraction length and speed calibration can improve print quality and achieve a clean, sharp print result. This subtle but essential detail in the printing process can distinguish between good and excellent results.

> Tip: Orca Slicer and other slicers offer calibration aids. You can also print retract tests here. However, remember that each filament from different manufacturers and different moisture levels produces different retracting behaviours.

Raft, Brim, Skirt

These three auxiliary structures improve the adhesion and stability of the print:

- The raft is a thick, removable base under the object

- The brim expands the first layer of the object to create more contact surface with the print bed

- The skirt (see also below) is a rim around the object that stabilises the filament flow before the actual print.

Tip: A brim only makes sense for small designs or designs with only a few edges on the print bed. If your design already has a lot of contact with the print bed, you don't need a brim. If you can't get such a motif to hold without a brim, there may be something wrong with your Z-offset, or your print bed is dirty.

Figure 15 5mm Brim surrounding print with Infill

Nozzle clog

Nozzle clogging occurs when foreign particles or burnt material block the filament flow, similar to a clogged tap. Regular cleaning and the use of high-quality filament can prevent this problem. Cheap filament in particular, sometimes has larger unclean areas than the 1.75 mm² diameter filament suitable for use. Small dents appear on the filament when large filament rolls are welded together during production. These are enough to clog the extruder and cause the print to fail. This is usually noticeable by a rapid clicking of the extruder. The gearbox tries to transport the filament, but it gets stuck. Your printer does not notice this, and the nozzle continues on its path. The filament just stops coming out.

TIP: Heat your printer at least 10 degrees above the usual printing temperature. You've likely received a small, fine, and long needle with your printer. Insert this from below to clear any blockages. Alternatively, at a higher temperature, you can try feeding new filament through. Be cautious, though—the extruder's gears might have already worn down some filament during unsuccessful feed attempts. It's a good idea to cut off about 10 cm from the front of the filament and discard it.

Skirt Lines

Your Slicer allows you to draw skirt lines around the whole (or also each single) motif. In my younger days, I refused to use these skirt lines as I thought of them as pure filament waste. But when you want to ensure from the first centimeter that your Z-Offset for the Print in Progress is the right one, then a few grams of Filament are no waste. Believe me.

Infill

Infill refers to the internal lattice structure that gives 3D prints stability and strength without wasting material. The density and pattern of the infill can be adjusted to find the ideal balance between strength and material usage. There are various types of infill patterns, each offering different benefits to support the durability of the print.

Tip: If the nozzle rattles when passing over the infill, it might be due to over-extrusion (too much filament being pushed out) or simply the infill pattern itself. The Gyroid infill is known for being both sturdy and particularly quiet during printing. I would suggest doing a flow calibration in the slicer and checking whether you have set the Z-hop. The Z-Hop lifts the print head slightly when it moves over the motif. Alternatively, you can also set the slicer so that the print head generally does not move over the motif but around it. It is a minor diversion that costs little time but gives a better print image.

Figure 16 4 of countless infill patterns

Print Fail

If someone tells you they haven't had a print fail this week, they've probably not even used their 3D printer yet. Mistakes happen, and they're simply part of the hobby. Don't get discouraged – every failure is an opportunity to learn something new.

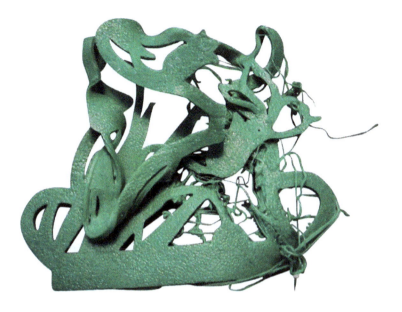

Figure 17 Of course, there are also print fails.

Z-Hop

Z-Hop is a 3D printing technique that aims to improve the quality of the printed product by reducing the risk of streaks and damage on the object's surface. With Z-hop, the print head (or Z-axis) is lifted slightly before moving to a new point on the print bed or over parts that have already been printed. This slight upward movement minimises the possibility of the print head or nozzle rubbing or sticking to the object's surface, resulting in a smoother surface and fewer irregularities in the finished product. Z-Hop is particularly useful when printing models with many protruding parts or overhangs. Although this technique can lead to slightly increased printing time, achieving a high-quality print result without unwanted marks or damage is often crucial.

!
Tip: Linked to the Z-Offset is a Slicer Setting where you can demand that the Nozzle not move above the motif or the support.

Klipper and Marlin

These two names appear again and again in consumer 3D printing. They are the firmwares with which consumer printers run. Older models or even cheaper models usually run with Marlin. Marlin is less demanding regarding computing power so that a cheaper mainboard can be installed in the printer. Sometimes, every cent counts in production. Higher quality or modern printers usually run with Klipper. Klipper is an open-source project and a fan project. It is a more powerful firmware that offers significantly more setting options than Marlin. But it also provides more possibilities to change something completely. With Klipper, you can optimise and calibrate your printer more precisely or entirely mess everything up. With the help of macros, you can install add-ons your manufacturer didn't think about when manufacturing your printer. My printers report their status every 10% via Discord with a picture. So, I always have an update, even when I'm on the move. It's an add-on that you can find on GitHub for free.

Klipper's limits lie solely in the fanbase's creativity. That's why many users convert their printers to Klipper with the help of a Raspberry.

To paraphrase a famous tale about a guidebook to the galaxy, just as a towel is an essential tool for any adventurer in space, understanding these specific terms is critical for anyone dedicated to 3D printing. And no matter how challenging your printing project may be, always respect the guiding principle of this universal guide. Don't panic!

The first steps with your FDM printer

Choosing the right printer

The journey into the world of 3D printing begins with choosing the right printer. This decision can be challenging due to the wide range of models available, each offering unique advantages. Factors like price, features, build volume, print speed, filament compatibility, and community support all play a critical role. For beginners, bed slinger models such as the Ender 3 from Creality, Anycubic's Kobra 3, or Elegoo's Neptune 4 Pro are excellent starting points. These Bed Slinger printers boast large communities, extensive documentation, and modding potential, making them ideal for those learning the ropes. For users seeking higher precision, faster speeds, or advanced features, CoreXY printers like the Qidi Plus 4 offer a compelling alternative. With their stationary bed design and efficient motion systems, CoreXY printers cater to enthusiasts ready to elevate their 3D printing experience. Both options empower users to take control of their printing journey, depending on their needs and aspirations.

CoreXY vs. Bed Slingers

When diving into 3D printing, you'll quickly discover that not all printers are created equal. Two of the most common types are CoreXY printers and bed slingers (Cartesian printers with a moving bed). Each has unique strengths, and understanding their differences can help you choose the best option for your needs—or appreciate the engineering behind each design.

A Tale of Two Designs

I've always been fascinated by the mechanical elegance of 3D printers. My actual love is a trusty bed slinger, the giant Elegoo Neptune 4 Max, which many hobbyists know and love. Its simplicity and affordability made it a perfect starting point. But when you try to do timelapse videos, you get into trouble moving this huge bed to park position each layer. Slight inaccuracies will happen. So, both systems have their place, but let me walk you through what makes them different.

The CoreXY Advantage: Speed, Precision, and Stability

CoreXY printers are built for speed and accuracy. Their design is fundamentally different from bed slingers. Instead of moving the bed back and forth, CoreXY printers keep it stationary or move it only on the Z-axis. This reduces the mechanical strain on the system and allows for faster, more precise movements.

Speed and Accuracy: Because only the print head moves in the X and Y axes, the CoreXY design minimises the weight and inertia of moving parts. This allows the printer to operate at higher speeds without compromising print quality.

Stable Print Bed: Have you ever printed a tall model on a bed slinger and noticed wobble lines or slight shifts in alignment? That's bed inertia at work. CoreXY printers avoid this entirely, as the bed doesn't move horizontally.

Compact Design: CoreXY mechanisms use a clever belt system that allows for a larger print volume within a smaller footprint. This is ideal if you're tight on space but want big prints.

Less Vibration: Because the heavy bed does not sling back and forth, CoreXY printers produce smoother surfaces and finer details.

Advanced Materials: Many CoreXY printers, come with enclosed designs. This makes printing advanced materials like ASA or ABS easier, which are sensitive to drafts and temperature fluctuations. The enclosure also prevents environmental factors like cold air or humidity from affecting your prints.

When I first used a CoreXY, I was surprised by how much of a difference a stationary bed made. The precision on the Y-axis was exceptional, allowing me to achieve details I hadn't thought possible on my bed slinger. It felt like an upgrade in hardware and the quality of my creative process.

Bed Slingers: The Workhorses of the 3D Printing World

That said, I'm not about to abandon my beloved Elegoo Neptune 4 Max. Bed slingers remain the backbone of many hobbyists' printing setups— and for good reason. They may not have the same speed or finesse as CoreXY printers, but their simplicity and affordability are hard to beat.

Affordable and Accessible: If you're new to 3D printing, bed slingers are a fantastic entry point. Their straightforward Cartesian mechanics keep costs low, making them accessible to beginners.

Easy Maintenance: With fewer complex components than CoreXY systems, bed slingers are easier to maintain and repair. Need to tighten a belt or replace a part? You'll likely find tutorials and spare parts with ease.

Customizability: Like the Neptune 4 Max, bed slingers are a modder's dream. From upgraded nozzles to enhanced firmware, these printers are highly customizable; for many users, it's part of the fun.

Troubleshooting Made Simple: Bed slingers' intuitive design makes diagnosing and fixing issues easier. If your prints start failing, you can quickly narrow the problem to the bed movement, the extruder, or other core components.

Wide Market Availability: Bed slingers dominate the market, which means you'll find a wealth of community support, accessories, and upgrades for models like the Neptune 4 Pro.

However, the moving bed does come with trade-offs. As the bed slings back and forth along the Y-axis, heavier or taller prints can introduce wobble or misalignment. This isn't a dealbreaker for most hobby projects, but it's something to consider if you print intricate or large-scale models.

My Experience with Both Worlds

While I've always appreciated the charm and reliability of my Neptune 4 Max and Neptune 4pro, the CoreXY bed brought a new level of precision to my prints. I noticed fewer artefacts, especially in taller models. The absence of a heavy bed moving along the Y-axis eliminated the slight misalignments I'd grown used to with bed slingers. The enclosed design was another game-changer, opening the door to experimenting with materials like ABS and ASA without worrying about drafts or uneven temperatures.

Still, I won't part with my Neptune 4 Max and Pro anytime soon. Its simplicity, affordability, and versatility make it perfect for quick projects or experiments. It's like having two tools in your workshop: one for precision work and one for dependable, everyday tasks.

Summary: Which One is Right for You?

If you're a beginner or hobbyist looking for a budget-friendly, easy-to-use printer, bed slingers are an excellent choice. It's straightforward, reliable, and widely supported.

If you're ready to take your 3D printing to the next level with faster speeds, higher precision, and the ability to work with advanced materials, a CoreXY printer is worth the investment.

Both designs have their strengths, and there's no one-size-fits-all answer. The best printer is the one that matches your needs, whether it's tinkering with a bed slinger or exploring the engineering elegance of a CoreXY. The good news? No matter your chosen path, you're stepping into a world of endless possibilities. Happy printing!

Setting up and preparing the printer

Most consumer printers today are manufactured in China. To avoid excessive transport costs, your printer comes as a kit with lots of screws and usually relatively poor instructions. Nevertheless, you should be able to assemble the printer in 30-60 minutes.

If you have ever assembled something with a screwdriver or Allen key, this should be easy, but, of course, all printers are mass-produced. So now is the time to check all the other pre-assembled screws. Are all the wheels firmly attached to the gantry, are the threaded rods for the Z-axis straight, and are all the control belts well-tightened? This avoids tedious troubleshooting afterwards.

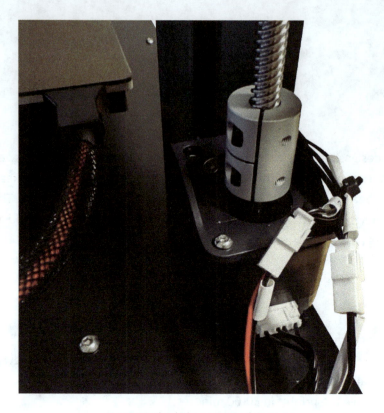

Figure 18 Check the position of the Z-axis

A friend once told me he tunes the belts like a good guitar string. Too loose, and the sound is crooked and too tight, and the string breaks.

It's similar to the belts in your printer. Too loose, and you will get messy outer walls or even a layer shift; too tight, and the belt will give way. If the instructions really don't help, search YouTube for tutorial videos from your printer manufacturer.

Eccentric Screws

Check all the wheels on the rails and the gantry. The wheels should roll smoothly but firmly on the rails without being too tight. Each carriage, usually consisting of three wheels, has one screw that is mounted eccentrically. This screw allows you to adjust the carriage. It's best to make this adjustment during assembly to prevent any issues with print quality later on.

Figure 19 Eccentric screws help with adjustment

Tool Kit

Every 3D printer comes with a small tool kit straight from the manufacturer. Unfortunately, the quality of these tools is often not the best. However, many online retailers now offer high-quality tools that are perfect for use with your 3D printer.

Figure 20 Tools and screws of a printer kit

Calibration

As already mentioned in this book, you should calibrate your new printer. Modern slicers offer many tools for this. There are countless tutorials on YouTube for every printer so that I won't mention every single calibration technique here. Every time I buy a new printer (which unfortunately happens more often because I'm a curious person 😊), I go through something like an initial installation routine. This ensures that I always have the perfect print for a long time. I'll list these points below for your guidance.

What do I calibrate first?

However, I will explain the steps in a little detail. The reason is quite simple. The types of calibration are simple, but each printer has its own peculiarities and may require different procedures. One example is the eccentric screws, which are present on most printers but are, of course, mounted in a different place. There are very good YouTube tutorials from the fanbase on every (and I believe really for every) printer. Find the experts for your printer and subscribe to their channels. Feel free to give a like for tutorials because that's the best reward, apart from sponsorship.

During assembly:

I check all the screws on the printer, especially those that are pre-assembled at the factory. As I said, the printer is manufactured quickly, so inattentive fitters are a realistic scenario.

If I find one or more screws that are turning noticeably, I look them up on the internet; not all screws on the printer have to be tight. For example, the screws that hold the Z-axis shaft on the Neptune 4 models from Elegoo. These need a bit of play.

I check all the wiring, my work, and the factory teams' work.

All moving parts are then greased well. The printers usually come with a small tube of grease. Otherwise, buy greases in the modelling shop that do not resinify. However, greasing well does not mean emptying the entire tube into one place.

Place the printer on a stable surface that does not wobble. I have usually fixed the tables on which the printer stands to the wall with several brackets. The printer may cause a table to vibrate, but not the wall.

Your printer does not like draughts or high humidity. Large temperature differences also influence the print result, especially if you print with more demanding materials than PLA. An unheated and poorly insulated garage may be an acceptable solution in summer, but in winter, it will affect the humidity of your PLA and, therefore, also the print results.

You finally want to print, and the printer software is already programmed with reasonable default settings at the factory. Get started and enjoy your first successes. But over time, you will see that you can always do a little bit better.

After assembly:

PID Tuning: The printer keeps your print head and heating bed at the temperature set in the slicer during printing. However, the temperature usually fluctuates around this value. The heating is switched on and off for the bed to maintain the value. Cold filament flows into the extruder, and the heating element has to react quickly. Temperature fluctuations are reduced if you do PID tuning for the bed and the extruder.

Flow rate: If your print image has uneven layers, the flow rate may be too high or too low. To avoid this, calibrate the flow rate.

Pressure Advance: Sometimes, your motif's corners and curves need to be cleaner. This may be because your printer needs to calculate more or less filament at this edge.

Retraction Test: If you look at the picture in this book about point stringing and see this in your print image, calibrate the retraction

- Max Volumetric Speed: I'll show you an example of how my Elegoo Neptune 4Max behaved ex-works.

Figure 21 Volume Flow Issue

The picture above shows that the printer could not print a full-coverage layer at maximum speed. The filament thread regularly broke off, and the image deteriorated with each layer above it. I read of many new starters who don't understand why their printer behaves as he does and how to fix it. You will receive the best print results possible if you calibrate your printer the best you can from day one.

In this example, the Maximum Volumetric Speed Test, in which the printer creates a pattern (see the image below), provided a remedy. Orca sets all the parameters, and after about 25 minutes and a few calculations with the calculator, I had the values at hand with which I could supply the printer (in the slicer, in this case) with the correct parameters. And I have to do this again with every filament. That's why having a particular brand loyalty to a filament manufacturer is recommended.

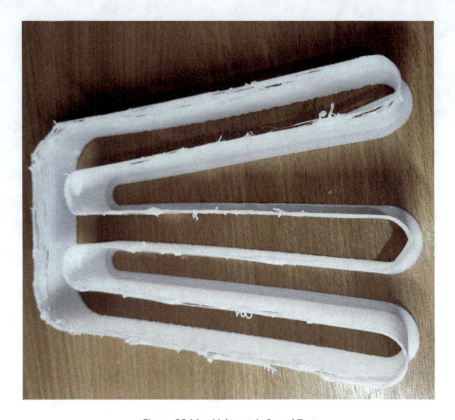

Figure 22 Max Volumetric Speed Test

I still have an older Elegoo Neptune 3pro in operation. It's not the fastest, but it's the most accurate. It is now running with an upstream Raspberry on Klipper (and got much faster by this). However, this printer had an inaccuracy, and a motif with an edge length of 1 cm had an edge length of 1.2 cm. If you now print a motif on several printers, the parts no longer fit. Or if you design a component that has to fit precisely somewhere. It didn't fit with the 3pro. The tolerance test helped here.

Once you have performed these calibrations, your printer will run optimally. Your slicer (e.g. Orca) will help you with most of these calibrations. You can find excellent tutorials on many of the topics on the Internet. Once you have done these routines, you will get even better results. But remember, a lot depends on the filament.

One example is the Temptower test. Here, you can determine how your filament prints at different printing temperatures. Does it tend to string at 220°C or only at 230°C? However, a different filament manufacturer or a higher humidity in the filament will cause your result to look different.

How to get an excellent first-layer

Levelling the print bed is a crucial step before the first print. A correctly levelled printing plate is a prerequisite for successful printing. Many printers now offer automatic levelling functions, but even here, a manual check can be good.

Always preheat your print bed to at least 60°C or the regular printing temperature your filament recommends. Once it has reached the target temperature, let the printer sit for a few minutes. The heat is typically measured in a central spot near the heating pad, but the edges of the bed might still only be at 45°C. So, wait until the entire bed has reached the correct temperature.

 Tip for the impatient: If you're about to print a model that will take several hours, 10 minutes for a well-levelled bed is time well spent. Only start the levelling process once the entire bed is heated correctly. Watch the process—there's something quite hypnotic about those smooth, steady movements.

Follow your printer's instructions to set the Z-offset, the distance between the nozzle and the print bed. This is important to ensure that the filament adheres properly to the bed. If the nozzle is too low, the filament will be squeezed out in wave-like patterns to the sides and will likely stick to the bed. However, due to the wavy filament pattern, the nozzle might rip off the first layer when printing the second one.

If the Z-offset is too high, the filament won't adhere to the print bed properly, and your entire print will eventually turn into a tangled mess of plastic trailing behind the nozzle. In the worst-case scenario, the first layer could detach just before the print finishes, wasting both filament and time.

 Tip: "If you think you have the Z-offset set correctly, you are still too high". This humorous but true saying emphasises the sensitivity required when setting the Z offset. It is advisable to start with a small test print to ensure the first layer adheres perfectly to the print bed.

The paper method is often recommended for setting the Z-offset. You enter the Z-offset mode in your printer's menu and place a sheet of paper between the nozzle and the print bed. Then, you lower the nozzle in 0.1 mm increments until you feel some resistance when moving the paper back and forth.

However, this is where the potential for error arises: How much resistance should there be? Are you using 80gsm or 60gsm paper? Is it matte or glossy? And if you have a bit of callus at your fingertips, everything might feel different.

Figure 23 How do I calibrate my Z-Offset

So, you can do this for a rough setting.

I recommend the following: I place a cube (see calibration section) on the print bed in the slicer (e.g., Cura) and scale it to the maximum print bed length and width but only 0.2 mm (i.e., one layer high). Then, I set the print speed to 50% and stand next to the printer. I observe the first layer and adjust the Z offset during printing.

A wavy pattern, for example, shows that the nozzle is too low, while gaps in the print show that the nozzle is too high. This certainly takes time until the process is complete, but then you have the perfectly adjusted bed. If you do not touch or move your printer, your Z-Offset should be stable.

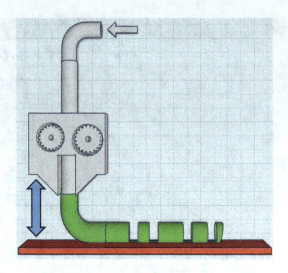

Figure 24 Z-Offset too high

If your Z-Offset (blue Arrow) is set too high, the nozzle cannot push the melted filament with the perfect strength into the print bed. Ultimately, the print may fail due to warping and bad adhesion.

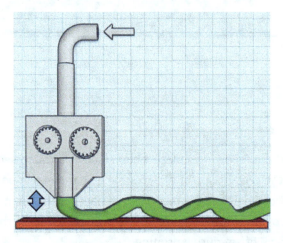

Figure 25 Z-Offset too low

If your Z-Offset (blue Arrow) is set too low, the nozzle will push the melted filament too deep into the print bed. The filament will swell and not lie flat on the bed. This may destroy the nozzle as it scratches the print bed. The Layer will look wavy, and while the nozzle prints the second layer, it might kick off the whole motif while touching and scratching the first layer.

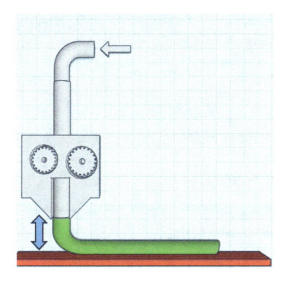

Figure 26 Z-Offset correct

You will achieve the perfect Z-Offset if you level your printer as described and print the recommended one-layer test cube while observing it. Your layers will stick to the print bed and look nice when the print is finished.

How fast to print?

So, most printers come with settings in a slicer. These are recommendations from either the Slicer Coder or the Printer Manufacturer. Nowadays, a printer is released faster than before each week. Is it good? Not always.

If you rush your first layer, how will it build up good adhesion? Change your Slicer Settings for the first layer, and push the break.

I print my first three layers in slow mode. I start Walls and Infill with 25mm²/sec and let the slicer automatically speed up to the maximum speed. You might spend only 30 minutes on three layers, but the math is simple compared to several failed prints, each ending after 20 minutes.

Mastering Key Slicer Settings for 3D Printing Success

Fine-tuning your slicer settings is one of the most critical steps in achieving high-quality 3D prints. While many printers offer good results with default settings, understanding and optimising essential parameters of your slicer can make the difference between a mediocre print and a professional-quality result. This chapter will explore 15 essential slicer settings, their impact on your prints, and how to use them effectively.

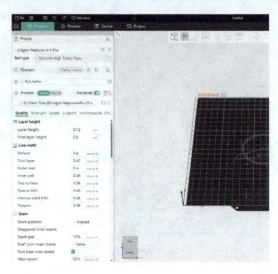

Figure 27 Settings in Orca Slicer

1. Layer Height

Layer height refers to the thickness of each individual layer in a print. It directly affects the level of detail, surface finish, and total print time.

- **Why It Matters:** Thinner layers (e.g., 0.1–0.2 mm) provide better detail and smoother curves but increase print time. Thicker layers (e.g., 0.3 mm or more) print faster but have a coarser finish.

- **Pro Tip:** Modern slicers like Orca or Cura include **adaptive layer height** settings. This feature adjusts the layer thickness dynamically to optimise curved surfaces, printing thinner layers for intricate areas and thicker ones for straight sections, striking the perfect balance between speed and quality. (see also next chapter)

2. Print Speed

Print speed determines how quickly the print head moves while extruding filament. It has a significant impact on both the print quality and the overall print time.

- **Why It Matters:** Faster speeds can reduce print times but may lead to lower surface quality or weak layer bonding. Slower speeds improve precision, especially with intricate models or small details.

- **Recommendation:** For general use, a speed of 50–60 mm/s works well. For fine details, reduce the speed to 30 mm/s or lower.

3. Nozzle Temperature

Nozzle temperature controls how well the filament melts and flows through the extruder. Each type of filament has an optimal temperature range.

- **Why It Matters:** Too low a temperature can cause poor adhesion or under-extrusion, while too high a temperature may lead to stringing or degraded material properties.

- **Pro Tip:** Always check the manufacturer's recommended temperature range for your filament.

4. Bed Temperature

The heated bed helps improve adhesion and prevent warping during printing, especially for materials prone to shrinkage, like ABS or PETG.

- **Why It Matters:** A properly heated bed ensures that the first layer adheres securely to the print surface, minimizing the risk of print failure.

- **Recommendation:** PLA prints well at 60 °C, while ABS and PETG may require 80–110 °C.

5. Infill Density

Infill density determines how much material fills the interior of your print. It plays a key role in balancing strength, weight, and material usage.

- **Why It Matters:** Higher infill density increases the strength and durability of the print but also uses more material and takes longer to print. Lower densities save time and material but may not provide enough structural support for functional parts.

- **Recommendation:** For general prints, use 20–40% infill. For highly stressed parts, consider 100% infill.

6. First Layer Settings

The first layer is the foundation of every successful print. Getting this layer right ensures stability and proper adhesion for the rest of the model.

- **Why It Matters:** Problems with the first layer, such as poor adhesion or uneven extrusion, can ruin an entire print.

- **Pro Tip:** For better adhesion, reduce the first layer speed to 20–30 mm/s and use slightly higher nozzle and bed temperatures than subsequent layers.

7. Build Plate Adhesion Type

Build plate adhesion settings, such as Skirt, Brim, or Raft, help ensure that the model adheres well to the bed.

- **Skirt:** A thin outline around the model, primarily used to prime the nozzle.

- **Brim:** Adds extra surface area around the model's base, improving adhesion for materials prone to warping.

- **Raft:** Creates a thick, flat base layer under the model, ideal for difficult materials or uneven beds.

- **Recommendation:** Use a Brim for warping-prone materials and a Skirt for simpler models where adhesion isn't a concern.

8. Retraction

During non-printing movements, retraction pulls the filament back into the nozzle to prevent oozing and stringing.

- **Why It Matters:** Without proper retraction settings, prints can suffer from unwanted strings or blobs of material.

- **Recommendation:** A retraction distance of 5–7 mm and a speed of 25–50 mm/s works well for most printers. TPU or flexible filaments may require lower settings.

9. Wall/Perimeter Thickness

Wall thickness refers to the number of perimeter lines or the total thickness of the outer shell.

- **Why It Matters:** Thicker walls provide more strength and a better surface finish, especially for functional parts.

- **Recommendation:** Use at least two perimeter lines or a minimum of 0.8 mm wall thickness for most prints.

10. Print Cooling

Cooling fans solidify the filament after extrusion, improving layer adhesion and surface finish.

- **Why It Matters:** Cooling is especially important for materials like PLA, which benefit from rapid cooling for clean, detailed prints. Conversely, materials like ABS require minimal cooling to avoid cracking or layer separation.

- **Recommendation:** Set cooling to 100% for PLA after the first layer and keep it minimal for ABS.

11. Top/Bottom Layers

The number of solid layers at the top and bottom of a print affects surface smoothness and structural integrity.

- **Why It Matters:** Too few top layers can result in visible infill patterns, while insufficient bottom layers can compromise the base's strength.

- **Recommendation:** Use 3–5 top and bottom layers for most prints. Increase this for models requiring smooth surfaces.

12. Support Settings

Supports are essential for overhangs or complex geometries where parts of the model lack a foundation.

- **Why It Matters:** Proper support settings ensure that overhanging sections are printed cleanly and without sagging.

- **Pro Tip:** Tree-style supports, available in many slicers, are easier to remove and use less material than traditional supports.

13. Extrusion Multiplier (Flow Rate)

This setting adjusts the amount of filament extruded, ensuring consistent flow and proper layer adhesion.

- **Why It Matters:** Under-extrusion leads to weak prints with gaps, while over-extrusion causes blobs and uneven layers.

- **Recommendation:** Keep the flow rate at 100% and make fine adjustments (e.g., ±1–2%) if needed.

14. Travel Speed

Travel speed governs how quickly the print head moves when not extruding material.

- **Why It Matters:** Faster travel speeds reduce stringing and save time but may introduce vibrations.
- **Recommendation:** Use speeds of 120–150 mm/s for most printers.

15. Z-Hop

Z-Hop lifts the nozzle slightly during travel moves to prevent it from dragging across the print.

- **Why It Matters:** Prevents scratches and collisions with already-printed parts.
- **Recommendation:** A 0.5–1 mm Z-Hop height is usually sufficient.

How to get an excellent last layer

If you print a rounded design, the layers at the top of the print may look uneven and not excellent, as in the picture below on the left. Your printer always prints with the same layer height that you have set in the slicer, probably 0.2 mm. But it would be best to have an intelligent layer height, especially for roundings. Many slicers have a function that helps you here. In the Orca Slicer, this function is called "Variable layer height" and can be found in the icon menu above your design. If you switch this function on, the slicer will determine which layer height will give you the best print result. It will then look like the image on the right.

Figure 28 Adaptive Layer Height

But this function improves printout quality and speed. The slicer also looks for areas where it can print with a layer thickness greater than 0.2 mm.

Below are two screenshots from the Orca Slicer, one with and one without the function switched on.

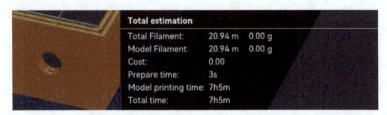

Figure 29 Adaptive layer height

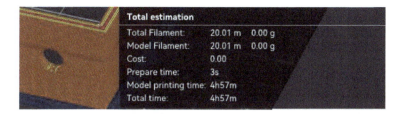

Total estimation		
Total Filament:	20.01 m	0.00 g
Model Filament:	20.01 m	0.00 g
Cost:	0.00	
Prepare time:	3s	
Model printing time:	4h57m	
Total time:	4h57m	

Figure 30 Saving Money and Time

Therefore, the Orca Slicer calculates a small layer height for the curves and goes to the maximum layer height for the straight surfaces without rounding, saving more than 2 hours of printing time and almost a whole metre of filament.

Where can I find models to print?

Before you can start printing, you need a model. Fortunately, there are a variety of online platforms where you can find free and paid 3D models. Thingiverse is one of the best-known websites and offers many models in various categories. MyMiniFactory is another excellent source known for its quality control and unique designs.

These websites are places to find models and communities where you can exchange ideas with other enthusiasts and share your creations.

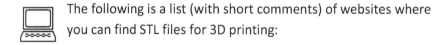

The following is a list (with short comments) of websites where you can find STL files for 3D printing:

- GrabCAD (https://grabcad.com/dashboard): An extensive community of professional engineers, manufacturers and designers who share a large selection of high-quality CAD files for

3D printing. Ideal for technical and complex projects.

- MyMiniFactory (https://www.myminifactory.com) offers a curated selection of 3D-printed models from a community of designers. The models are guaranteed printable and often categorised by theme, ideal for hobbyists and creative users.

- It'sLitho (https://tool.itslitho.com/) Specializes in creating lithophanes, images engraved into thin plates and then transilluminated. It is a unique tool for personalised and artistic print projects. The book also contains a few words about this.

- Pinshape (https://pinshape.com/) is a market platform that offers a variety of STL files for 3D printers. The community shares free and paid designs covering a wide range of interests.

- Yeggi (https://www.yeggi.com/): A search engine for 3D print models that searches multiple databases. Ideal for getting a quick overview of the available designs and finding the perfect model for your next project.

- STLFinder (https://www.stlfinder.com/) is another powerful tool for finding STL files. It searches the websites of several providers, a good starting point for a comprehensive search.

- Thangs (https://thangs.com/): A relatively new but rapidly growing platform that provides a geometric search engine for finding and sharing 3D models. It makes it possible to find similar models based on geometric shapes.

- Cults (https://cults3d.com): A digital marketplace for 3D print files that offers designs from independent designers. Here, you will find both free and commercial designs for various applications.

- Printables (https://www.printables.com): Run by Prusa Research, this website offers free STL files that can be printed in high quality. It is especially recommended for owners of Prusa printers.

- Nametag Designer (https://www.nametag-designer.com): Specialising in personalised name tags, it offers an intuitive tool for quickly creating and printing custom designs.

- Thingiverse (https://www.thingiverse.com) is one of the oldest and most popular portals for free STL files. It offers an enormous variety of designs for practically any idea.

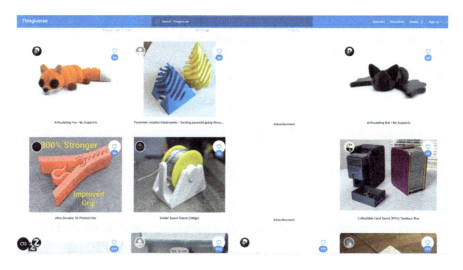

Figure 31 Thingiverse, an excellent Search Engine for your favourite STL Files

- Makeronline (https://www.makeronline.com) is a platform from Anycubic on which many colourful designs for the Kobra 3 Combo are also available.

As you can see, almost every 3D printer manufacturer has their open platform. However, since the STL format is the universal standard for most consumer 3D printers, you can easily print a model from Yeggi on an Anycubic printer or a Prusa model on a Sovol printer. Don't worry—give it a try!

Can I print a Bambulab design on my Anycubic printer?

The answer is yes. When you load an STL file from a portal into your slicer, it turns into a universal GCODE file, which you load into your printer via browser or USB stick. If you receive a file as a print profile (3MF) from the Internet, the creator of the file has already stored the best print parameters - for his printer. You must, therefore, be careful here and select the print parameters of your printer again in the slicer. In the end, however, you will also receive a GCODE file to load into your printer.

Initial print settings and tests

Once you have selected your model, it is time to adjust the print settings in your slicing software. The optimal setting depends on many factors, including the chosen material, the complexity of the model and the desired print quality. The community-recommended settings for your specific printer and filament are a good starting point. Start with simple models to get a feel for the settings

Summary

Taking your first steps in the world of 3D printing is exciting, but it can also be a steep learning curve. Choosing the right printer, setting up and preparing the printer, levelling the print bed, and selecting your first model are all important steps on the road to successful 3D printing. With patience, practice, and a willingness to learn from the community, you can soon create your own impressive 3D prints.

When delving into the depths of advanced printing methods, it's impossible not to be overwhelmed by the numerous technological marvels and innovations that a legendary space saga has sparked in our imagination. One striking example is a certain spherical droid, a true marvel of robotics that plays a key role in a galaxy far away and in the hearts of its followers. The challenge of creating a model of this droid using modern printing techniques not only serves as a challenging test of your 3D printing skills but also highlights the strong link between the creative potential of 3D printing and the inspiring world of the aforementioned space fairy tale. The successful realization of such a complex model requires masterful handling of support structures and precise control over hanging parts. It is particularly challenging due to its unique spherical shape and detailed components.

Using the spherical droid and the world of the epic space tale as a source of inspiration, we remember that the limits of our creativity are only limited by our own imagination. This interstellar epic has inspired generations to think and dream beyond the seemingly impossible. Similarly, 3D printing motivates us to push the boundaries of what is possible and create objects that once existed only in the realms of science fiction. Just as the engineers and designers in the saga urge us to embrace technology and use it for the good of the galaxy, 3D printing challenges us to unleash our creative power and shape realities that mirror our wildest dreams and visions. May the creative force be with you!

Understanding the printing materials

Introduction to the world of filaments

Materials play a central role in 3D printing. Choosing the right filament can make the difference between a mediocre and an excellent print result. In this chapter, we explore the world of filaments, from the most commonly used materials, such as PLA and PETG, to speciality filaments for specific requirements.

PLA: The environmentally friendly favourite

PLA, or polylactide, is the favourite material of many 3D printing enthusiasts due to its ease of use and environmental friendliness. It is biodegradable and made from renewable resources, making it an excellent choice for general printing projects. PLA is particularly suitable for beginners as it requires a lower printing temperature than other materials and is less prone to warping.

From my observations, the difference between PLA, high-speed PLA, PLA+, and whatever they are all called is insignificant. And I suspect it's more of a marketing gimmick for higher margins than an evident added value. Remember that the faster you print, the more you might go to the upper limit of the allowed temperature to help your printhead deliver the needed Filament Volume.

I have my favourite filament manufacturer, and I buy from them. But even I can only sometimes resist special offers on eBay or AliExpress. So far, 95% of my purchases have turned out well.

I met a nice Filament Supplier at the last Fairs. Rosa3D Filaments is from Poland (https://www.rosa3d.pl/) and has excellent quality and fantastic colour combinations like Fluo, Rainbow, and many more.

Figure 32 Rosa3D Logo

Due to their location in Poland, their delivery Time in Europe is relatively fast, but if you live outside of Europe, you can find them on Amazon. If you, like me, like to support smaller and local companies, check their products.

! Tip: Modern high-speed consumer printers must melt the filament quickly and transfer it to the print bed. In my experience, the temperatures stated on the stickers on the filament roll have nothing to do with reality. I set the slicer so that it heats the filament to 225°C. So far, I have achieved good results with most manufacturer.

But please don't look for every fault in yourself. In the picture below, you can see two Raspberry camera holders I designed in Fusion360 and printed one after the other on the same machine (Elegoo Neptune 4max) with the same settings. One Filament was a 2.5 kg NoName roll, and the other was a Jayo filament. The result surprised even me. Since then, I've only used the 2.5 kg roll for quick prototypes where I don't care about the quality and only want to check the dimensions.

Figure 33 Printfails are not always your fault

PETG: PLA's robust friend

PETG, an acronym for polyethene terephthalate with added glycol, is a robust and versatile filament valued in the world of 3D printing for its ease of use and excellent printing properties. It combines the lightness and clarity of PET, as used in water bottles, with an additional glycol component that reduces brittleness and increases toughness. PETG is characterised by high impact resistance, clarity and odourless printing. It adheres well to the print bed and is more resistant to temperature fluctuations, which reduces warping. The material is also resistant to many chemicals and can be sterilised, making it suitable for medical applications and food packaging. However, PETG can be demanding in printing conditions and requires careful print speed and extrusion temperature balancing to achieve optimal results. There are machines made by 3D printing enthusiasts that turn a PET drinking bottle into a printable filament. However, the risk of nozzle clogging must always be taken into account.

 TIP: PETG needs to be printed slightly differently than PLA. I print PETG at about 60% of the speed at which I print PLA. I also like to increase the temperature to 250°C so it flows better. Of course, printing now takes significantly longer than with PLA, but the reward is a much more stable component.

ABS: Strong and resistant

ABS, or acrylonitrile butadiene styrene, is another popular filament known for its robustness and heat resistance. It is the material of choice for projects requiring higher mechanical strength, such as functional parts or objects exposed to heat. However, ABS requires higher printing temperatures and a heated plate to avoid warping. In addition, when printing with ABS, the temperature in the room must always remain constant. Therefore, you should never use ABS without an enclosure around your printer.

Speciality filaments: Expand your possibilities

In addition to PLA and ABS, various speciality filaments have been developed for specific applications. These include flexible filaments for flexible objects, wood filler filaments for a wood-like surface and many others. Each of these materials has unique properties and requires specific print settings. TPU, or thermoplastic polyurethane, is a flexible and stretchable filament prized in the 3D printing community for its elasticity and durability. The rubber-like material is resistant to oil, grease and abrasion. It is, therefore, ideal for applications where flexibility and shock absorption are required, such as mobile phone covers, shoe soles or seals. TPU combines the advantages of plastics and silicones by being dimensionally stable and flexible, making it a favoured material for functional moving parts and objects with complex geometries. However, care must be taken when printing with TPU, as its flexibility places unique demands on the extruder and requires optimised print settings to achieve the best possible results. A Bowden extruder is barely capable of processing TPU. It's like trying to push a cooked spaghetti up a straw. Good luck.

Tip: As mentioned above, every manufacturer and every filament has different properties. Sometimes, all you need to do is change the colour of the same manufacturer, and you will get a different print result. Silk filaments look very nice but will behave differently on your printer than standard colours. It's best to choose a manufacturer you like to print with and then print a component from the calibration tools in the slicer once with each PLA. As a nice side effect, you will also have a collection of leftover samples with the printed colours and can later judge whether the red has the right shade as the other one.

Filament Type	Bed Temp	Filament Temp	Pro	Con
PLA	60°C-70°C	190°C-225°C	Low cost, easy to print, plenty of colours	low resistance to heat and impact, tends to get humid and then get brittle and break
PETG	80°C-90°C	230°C-250°C	stronger and more heat resistant than PLA	Tends to string and bad bridging characteristics
TPU	45°C-60°C	225°C-250°C	Flexible and soft	Difficult to print, slow print only, tends to stringing
ABS	90°C-110°C	220°C-250°C	Good Impact and wear resistance	Needs heated chamber, shrinks heavily
ASA	90°C-110°C	220°C-250°C	Strong UV Resistant, high impact resistant	Expensive, needs ventilation due to dangerous fumes
Wood, Metal, Marmor filled Filament	60°C-70°C	190°C-225°C	mostly based on PLA	can be abrasive and therefore damage the nozzle on a long run

So, how to set the proper Filament temperature on your slicer? First of all, there are recommendations from the filament manufacturer for each coil. Secondly, the faster your printer extrudes, the more fluid the filament needs to be. If you overheat it, the filament will ooze out of the nozzle and damage your final result; if you are too low, your extruder might not be able to deliver the filament fast enough. And again, each manufacturer's filament might need a different setting. So easy, huh?

According to the bed temperature, I learned that I slice the first layer always 10°C above the recommended temperature. Meaning, if you print with PLA, your Bed Temperature should be 60°C in general and 70°C for the first layer. That helped me improve the bed adhesion.

Filament storage: a key to success

One of the most overlooked elements of 3D printing is proper filament storage. Filaments attract moisture from the air, which can lead to printing problems. Dry storage in airtight containers with silica gel packets can significantly extend filament life and improve print quality.

Moist filament is particularly prone to stringing, breaks more easily, provides a messy print image, and ensures that layers do not form a smooth outer wall. These errors can occur but do not necessarily have to be the result. Nevertheless, many questions in forums where unclean print images are shown can often be traced back to wet filament.

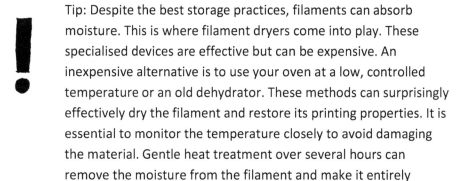

Tip: Despite the best storage practices, filaments can absorb moisture. This is where filament dryers come into play. These specialised devices are effective but can be expensive. An inexpensive alternative is to use your oven at a low, controlled temperature or an old dehydrator. These methods can surprisingly effectively dry the filament and restore its printing properties. It is essential to monitor the temperature closely to avoid damaging the material. Gentle heat treatment over several hours can remove the moisture from the filament and make it entirely usable again.

Figure 34 Mum's good old dehydrator

Summary

The filaments world is diverse and offers unlimited possibilities for your 3D printing projects. The right choice and care of your filaments can significantly impact the quality of your prints. From knowing the different materials to proper storage and drying, every detail counts on the way to the perfect print. In this chapter, we've covered the basics you need to be on the safe side when choosing materials and getting the best results from your 3D printer. Amidst the technical details and practical tips on filaments, a little anecdote from the popular science fiction series "Futurama" reminds us just how close the future really is. In one episode, Professor Farnsworth proudly presents a "Matter Compiler" that can create almost anything from nothing - a fascinating notion that doesn't seem far removed from the reality of 3D printing today. Like Farnsworth's inventions, often presented with humour and a dash of ingenuity, the various filaments used in 3D printing open up a world of creative and sometimes surprising possibilities.

The evolution of advanced 3D printing technologies

In the dynamic field of 3D printing, advanced technologies mark the beginning of an era in which the boundaries of creativity and technical feasibility are constantly redefined. Beyond the basics that provide a solid introduction to this ground-breaking technology, innovative processes allow for a reinterpretation of design and manufacturing conventions. Based on exceptional precision and detail, these methods enable the production of objects whose complexity and quality far exceed what could be achieved using traditional methods.

Fine-tuning at a molecular level

At the heart of advanced 3D printing technologies lies the constant pursuit of perfecting print quality. This goal requires a comprehensive understanding of the complex dynamics between print speed, temperature control and cooling mechanisms. Careful tuning of these variables can result in remarkable refinement of surface texture, render overhangs with incredible accuracy and improve the structural integrity of the printed object. Experts invest tireless hours of research into optimising these settings for different materials and specific models to achieve peak performance. The realisation that increasing print speed can save time but often comes at the expense of accuracy and final quality underlines the importance of these fine adjustments.

The strategic role of support structures

Support structures play a crucial role in the extended range of 3D printing. They are essential for successfully realising models with significant overhangs or complex geometries that would otherwise not be feasible in the printing process. The trick is to design and place these supports to fulfil their purpose without compromising the final product or requiring extensive post-processing. Modern slicer programs offer increasingly sophisticated ways to precisely control the placement and density of support structures, which significantly improves print results.

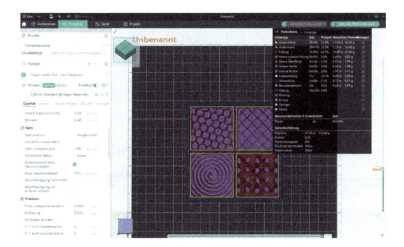

Figure 35 Orca Slicer – one of several Slicers

Imagine you want to attach a balcony to your house. To do this, you erect scaffolding during assembly. This scaffolding stabilises the construction process until it is complete and the balcony firmly attaches to your home.

It's the same in the 3D world. A printer can arrange the filament up to a certain angle to remain in the structure. If the overhang is too large, the filament falls to the floor like hot spaghetti, and you have another fail.

Two support structures have been established for private users in 3D printing. A standardised one that is attached like a fan under your design. After printing, you remove the structure. The advantage: It is quickly created for the printer and relatively stable thanks to its structure. The disadvantage: Sometimes, a structure has to be built on top of material that has already been printed. When the texture is removed, unsightly residues are usually left behind. You have to rework with sandpaper.

Figure 36 Remnants of support structures

The second support structure is the so-called tree structure. Here, the print bed builds up many small branches that only touch the print image where necessary. The many branches look interesting, sometimes almost more interesting than the motif itself. Disadvantage: More filament is used than with the classic structure, and the many small branches are more susceptible to breakage and, therefore, harbour the risk of another failure. Advantage: With the correct planning, the tree supports leave almost no residue on the motif and can, thus, also be used for complicated works.

Figure 37 When the supports are scarier than the motif-tree supports

Expanding the colour palette: multicolour printing

The ability to produce objects in multiple colours or materials in a single printing process represents a revolutionary expansion of creative horizons. This complex technique requires specialised hardware, such as printers with multiple extruders or multiple Filament Feeders and a deep understanding of material properties and their interaction during printing. The challenge is to select and combine the materials to create a harmonious overall picture without compromising the structural or aesthetic quality. This technology opens up previously unimaginable possibilities for innovative projects that set new standards in personalisation and functionality, but new dangers and challenges are lurking here. Multicolour printers with only one hotend and one extruder generate large amounts of waste, and the effect of colour bleeding occurs with incorrect settings.

While I write this book, I run an Anycubic Kobra3 Combo with two ACE pro, allowing me to print eight colours in one print. An ACE pro is a Filament dryer for 4 Spools that allows changing the Filament Colour or Type (PLA to PETG) in one layer.

The advantage is clear: no more painting after printing.

The disadvantage of this technology that several manufacturers use is that the printer must clear the nozzle each time you change the colour. This can lead to hundreds of filament changes where the printer "poops out" the filament used before. I don't think this kind of technology for colour prints will still exist in 5 to 10 years, but for the moment, it's fun.

Prusa and a few others take another way, building several extruders in one printer. This increases the price and limits your colour prints to the number of extruders. For the Anycubic, I bought another ACE Pro and extended the printer from 4 to 8 colours.

Inspired by the limitless possibilities and technological masterpieces presented by a specific legendary space series, advances in 3D printing show how the boundaries of what is possible are constantly being redefined. Like fictional engineers who use their advanced equipment to create objects virtually out of thin air, 3D printing allows us to merge imagination and reality. From the perfect replica of a famous spaceship to functional objects that could be straight out of a TV series, 3D printing brings the future closer to us. Advanced 3D printing technologies - from the meticulous fine-tuning of printing parameters to the intelligent use of support structures and the ground-breaking introduction of multi-colour and multi-material printing - open up a universe of creative possibilities. These techniques require patience, precision and the courage to push known boundaries - qualities that characterise the pioneers of 3D printing and the visionary characters of our favourite science fiction stories.

Post-processing 3D prints

Post-processing is an essential step in the 3D printing process that is often overlooked but can turn a good project into something extraordinary. In this chapter, we focus on the different techniques you can use to improve the quality and appearance of your prints, with a particular emphasis on airbrushing. It will also introduce you to a second new hobby.

Why post-processing? Post-processing can help improve surface quality, enhance aesthetic appeal and even strengthen the structural integrity of the printed object. From simple sanding and polishing to complex painting, finishing can personalise your prints and make them stand out from standard prints. Basic finishing techniques include sanding to achieve a smooth surface, removing support structures, gluing multi-part prints together, and priming in preparation for painting. These steps form the basis for further finishing techniques.

The essential finishing techniques include sanding to achieve a smooth surface, removing support structures, glueing multi-part prints together and priming in preparation for painting. These steps form the basis for further finishing techniques.

Airbrushing is an art that requires precision and patience, but the results can be stunning. With an airbrush kit, you can add fine details, create colour gradients and give your prints a realistic look

- Preparation: Careful preparation is vital. The surface should be clean, smooth and primed

- Technique: Start with a practice area. Hold the airbrush at a constant angle and work in thin layers.

- Colour mixing and application: Experiment with colour blends and use masking techniques for specific patterns.

Other finishing techniques

In addition to airbrushing, numerous other techniques exist, such as hand painting for fine detail and applying weather effects for an aged look. The refinement of replicas reminiscent of legendary equipment and companions from a galaxy far away, such as elegant energy weapons or faithful mechanical companions, emphasises the importance of precise finishing methods. Known for their intricate detail and colour gradients, these recreations require a mastery of airbrushing techniques to appear authentic - comparable to the meticulous design of film sets. Visualise perfecting your own model of a famous freighter, complete with every tiny trace of use and the signs of space battles.

Troubleshooting, maintenance and improvements

The 3D printing process is complex and requires a deep understanding of the machine and the material. Problems can occur, but these challenges can be overcome with the proper knowledge and the support of an active community. In this chapter, we dive deeper into troubleshooting, examine the maintenance of your printer and how upgrades can improve quality and user experience. Deeper failure analysis Failing prints are not only frustrating but also educational. In the 3D printing community, it's common to share images of misprints to analyse together what went wrong. This open discussion often leads to valuable insights and solutions. Showing misprints is encouraged in many forums and Discord servers, as it is a vital learning resource for all involved.

Regular maintenance

Your printer is a high-performance device. Speeds of up to 5000mm/s are not uncommon these days. I always call my printers sewing machines on drugs. And that's precisely how it needs to be treated. Lubricate or oil all moving parts regularly - even once a week, depending on the print. Use oils or greases that are not resinous or sticky. There are better solutions than salad oil from the kitchen. Use oils like those used for model railways or the sound old Slot Car track. Regular maintenance is crucial for the performance of your 3D printer.

Recommended routines include:

- Cleaning the printing plate to ensure optimal adhesion

- Lubricating the axes: For smooth movement

- Checking and replacing wearing parts: Nozzle and PTFE tube to ensure consistent print quality.

This is the most essential part of your 3D printing experience. If you are not very precise here, you may not enjoy 3D printing.

As you can see from the various photos, I have Elegoo 3D printers in my workshop.

Figure 38 Elegoo Logo

Why? In my "career" as a 3D printing fan, I have owned various printers from different generations and manufacturers. I am convinced that while you read that book, I already think about a new printer.

My close relationship with Elegoo (www.elegoo.com) has resulted from my experiences with other manufacturers.

My best perception was the combination of workmanship, customer service and spare parts supply. But don't start a fundamental discussion about brands and printer manufacturers in the social media groups mentioned in this book. It will be a never-ending story.

 Elegoo runs a very open Discord server (https://discord.gg/4YJjjRbh), encouraging the fanbase to replace the factory firmware with an alternative (possibly better) firmware. I have rarely discovered a manufacturer that is so close to open source. The service responds within 24 hours from China, delivering spare parts quickly. Elegoo gives away monthly gifts (e.g. printers) on its Discord server to reward users who are very involved in the community. Even basic improvements to devices are rewarded.

Currently, at a time when more manufacturers are switching to plastic gantries to produce even more cheaply, Elegoo still relies on metal gantries. I hope it stays that way.

Figure 39 The small print corner with Elegoo Neptune 4max, Neptune 3pro, Neptune 4pro

But no matter which manufacturer you choose, make sure you find out before you call for help in any forums - always remember the PEBCAK error. Among IT technicians and software developers, this is an abbreviation for "Problem exists between Chair and Keyboard," although in the 3D printer market, it should undoubtedly be called PEBCAP. 😅

Improving the printer

Many enthusiasts strive to improve their printers through hardware upgrades or firmware adjustments.

- Hardware upgrades: Replacing parts or adding new components can improve print quality, speed and the overall experience. Examples include switching to a direct-drive extruder for better handling of flexible filaments or upgrading to quieter stepper motors for quieter operation.

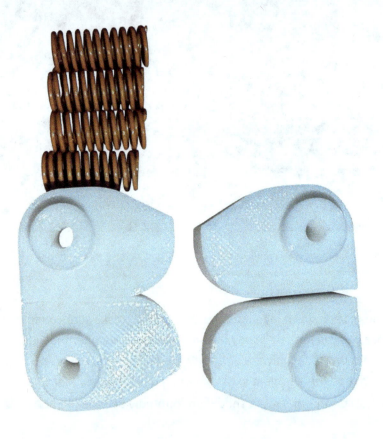

Figure 40 Why not give your printer an upgrade and replace the overly soft springs with self-printed TPU dampers

- Firmware changes: Changing or updating a 3D printer's firmware can unlock new features and boost performance. Popular firmware such as Marlin or Klipper offers advanced customisation options and can help increase the printer's precision and speed.

When you check the picture of my printers (above) you might recognise that none has their initial display anymore. I moved all of them to a clear and unchanged Klipper Firmware.

This brought my Neptune 3pro almost to the speed of the Neptune 4pro. This means I upgraded an older Printer with new firmware to the level of a new printer. In addition, all my printers are running with Klipper Screen, allowing me to better fine adjust them and control prints better than the manufacturer's display would allow me to do.

Tools like Klipper Screen can be found on GitHub (see below). This is one of hundreds of open-source projects available there. Although they may be available free of charge, the coder always likes to get a cup of coffee.

The power of the community The 3D printing community is an invaluable resource for support and inspiration. Many manufacturers and software developers run active Discord servers or forums where users can ask questions, share knowledge and discuss best practices - Community support: Whether you need help with troubleshooting, advice on upgrades or want to share your latest creations, there's always someone willing to help. This mutual support is invaluable not only for beginners but also for experienced users.

Figure 41 Discord Logo

Summary

Troubleshooting and maintenance are essential in 3D printing, but a willingness to improve and customise can significantly improve your skills and the quality of your prints. Community support and the sharing of experiences are essential. Regular maintenance, a willingness to analyse errors and striving for improvements will ensure the longevity of your printer and take your 3D printing projects to the next level. In a famous galactic research series, the speed with which challenges are responded to and creative solutions developed is a characteristic feature of the onboard technicians. From the legendary words of a Scottish engineer assuring his captain that he is doing all he can to the technical feats of a brilliant chief engineer at the heart of a famous next-generation research vessel, these problem-solving moments are inspiring. They encourage us to recognise that every misprint and technical difficulty is an opportunity for innovation and learning, much like the crew of that famous ship coming together around a table to find solutions to seemingly unsolvable tasks. Within the 3D printing community, we cultivate this spirit of collaboration, sharing our knowledge, supporting each other and growing together. Do you also feel inspired by the "research fleet mentality" to make the impossible possible? Beam me up, 3D printer!

Design software and resources

A comprehensive guide Design is the first and one of the most crucial steps on the journey from idea to finished 3D print. Choosing the right tools and resources is vital. This chapter introduces you to CAD software and shows how online resources and communities can enhance the design and printing process. An in-depth look at CAD software: CAD software is the backbone of 3D printing design. These programs enable the creation of complex and precise models that can then be converted into real objects, from entry-level programs such as Tinkercad, which impresses with its intuitive user interface, to professional applications such as Fusion

360 or SolidWorks, which offer extensive tools for detailed designs and technical drawings. Free vs. commercial software: a detailed analysis The choice between free and commercial software depends on many factors, including your specific design requirements, budget and the size of your projects. While programs such as Blender and SketchUp offer excellent free options for designers looking to enter the world of 3D printing, commercial software packages such as AutoCAD provide additional features that may be required for specific industries or professional applications. In this section, we explore the strengths and weaknesses of both options and offer guidelines on how to make the best choice for your projects.

Tinkercad

Tinkercad, an Autodesk product, is a user-friendly, web-based application designed to help beginners enter the world of 3D design. With its intuitive drag-and-drop interface, Tinkercad enables users of all ages and abilities to create three-dimensional objects in minutes. From simple pieces of jewellery to complex models for 3D printing, Tinkercad offers a wide range of tools and templates to encourage creativity. In addition, Tinkercad also supports circuit design and microcontroller programming, making it a versatile tool for hobbyists and educational institutions. Its accessibility and simplicity make Tinkercad a popular choice for entering the digital design and prototyping world.

Figure 42 Tinkercad Logo

Fusion360

Fusion 360, also from Autodesk, is a robust and comprehensive computer-aided design (CAD) software. It offers seamless integration of various design and engineering processes on a single cloud-based platform that is available free of charge to both professional designers and hobbyists. With Fusion 360, users can create complex 3D models, run simulations to test functionality and resilience and prepare tool paths for manufacturing. The software supports real-time collaboration, allowing teams to develop and work on projects regardless of location. Fusion 360 is viral in product design, mechanical design and engineering, offering a flexible and efficient solution to modern design and manufacturing challenges.

TIP: I started my journey into 3D design with Tinkercad and quickly created my first small designs. But at some point, you reach a limit and start looking for more possibilities. I wanted to design, print and give away illuminated 3D name lamps. And I had no idea. So I watched tutorials on YouTube and eventually met a few new friends on Discord, one of whom had already designed these lamps. He taught me, and I took my first steps in Fusion360. If I notice something missing in my house, car, etc., I design it in Fusion360 and print it out.

Figure 43 Fusion 360 Logo

Online resources and communities: more than just models

As mentioned, the internet is a treasure trove for 3D printing enthusiasts. In addition to model libraries such as Thingiverse and MyMiniFactory, which offer a wealth of ready-to-print models, online communities and forums are indispensable for exchanging knowledge and experience.

Platforms such as Reddit, specialised forums, and Discord servers offer direct access to a community of like-minded people. Users' sharing of experiences with misprints is particularly appreciated here. This promotes a culture of learning and continuous improvement. The open exchange of challenges and solutions can greatly help, especially for those new to 3D printing.

But please remember one thing before asking a question that has already been answered a million times: GIYF—Google is your friend. I often read the same question four times a day on a Facebook group. And for sure, at some point, the experts will react annoyed, and you will not be happy as you did not receive the support you hoped to receive. So please read yourself in before asking.

Sharing Designs and Insights

The 3D printing community emphasises design sharing and collaboration. Many designers use platforms to showcase their work and receive feedback, encouraging the iterative design process. This section promotes active participation in this culture of sharing and collaboration. By publishing your designs or participating in discussions about design improvements, you can help others and develop your skills.

The synergy between futuristic narratives and advanced printing technology extends far beyond a mere enthusiasm for technology. It illustrates how today's tools can open the door to the future. One captivating endeavour could be to recreate legendary objects from epic space adventures, where characters such as a (limited) speaking, tree-like hero blur the line between imagination and reality. These projects illustrate what is possible with current printing technology and emphasise how design software allows us to turn even our wildest visions into reality. How would you feel about creating your own versions of such incredible artefacts? Perhaps it is a sign that we are not too far away from realising our most fantastical sci-fi dreams

Summary

This chapter has provided a detailed insight into the selection and use of design software in the 3D printing process, emphasising the importance of online resources and the power of the community. With the right tools and community support, you can develop the skills to turn your ideas into reality and become part of a global movement fuelled by creativity and innovation.

Environmental aspects of 3D printing

3D printing has revolutionised product manufacturing and design but also brings unique challenges and opportunities regarding sustainability and environmental protection. We can minimise our projects' environmental footprint by avoiding waste, using biodegradable materials, and optimising printing processes.

This section emphasises the importance of conscious resource use and provides an overview of the most crucial sustainability principles in 3D printing. Choosing environmentally friendly filaments plays a decisive role in the environmental impact of 3D printing. PLA (polylactide) is a popular choice for environmentally conscious users as it is biodegradable and made from renewable resources such as corn starch.

Other bio-based filaments, such as PETG (modified polyethylene terephthalate), offer similar benefits and more outstanding durability. This section provides a detailed comparison of eco-friendly filament options and their potential uses. Recycling and reusing 3D printing waste, an essential element of sustainability in 3D printing, is minimising and recycling material waste. From reusing support material and misprints to shredding and extruding waste into new filaments, there are many ways to close the material loop. We explore different methods and technologies that enable recycling in your own workshop or office.

Environmentally friendly practices in 3D printing In addition to material selection and recycling, there are many other steps that individuals and organisations can take to make their 3D printing processes more environmentally friendly. These include energy efficiency, optimising print design to save material and getting involved in local recycling schemes.

In the universe of a famous animated film set on an abandoned Earth, a small clean-up robot impressively demonstrates the importance of recycling and careful resource management. This robot, which creates something unforgettable from a mountain of waste, illustrates the consequences of overconsumption and waste while inspiring us with its tireless commitment and creativity in using recyclable materials. This narrative encourages us to make a difference in tackling environmental issues through mindful choices and innovation - a principle that applies to eco-friendly 3D printing.

The path from design to print

Congratulations. You have now learned many details about 3D printing. But how do you mould the filament on the print bed? The transition from a 3D model to a physical object is fascinating. The selection of suitable file formats, the optimisation of the slicing process, and the efficient transfer of the files to the printer characterises it.

This chapter provides an overview of these critical steps, prepares for a more in-depth look at firmware in the next chapter, and highlights the magical connection between 3D printing and science fiction.

3D printing basics

3D printing turns digital designs into tangible objects through additive manufacturing, where the material is applied layer by layer. The process begins with a 3D model, typically created in a CAD program and then converted into a printable format.

STL and G-code

The languages of 3D printing - STL files: STL stands for "Stereolithography" or "Standard Tessellation Language" and is the most commonly used format for 3D print designs. These files describe the surface of 3D models using triangles. A significant advantage of STL files is that they are compatible with almost all 3D printing programmes. However, they only represent the outer shape of the object without colour or material information - G-code files: After an STL model has been sliced, it is converted into G-code, the language that 3D printers understand. These files contain detailed instructions for the printer, including movements, speeds and temperatures. G-code is the end product of the slicing process and the direct link between your design and the physical print.

 Tip: I often read in forums that a beginner tries to transfer a motif to the printer using an SD card, but the motif is not visible on the printer display. Now, many people despair. Most of the time, the user has loaded the STL file onto the SD card. In other words, the unsliced motif. However, the printer cannot read the STL format. It must include essential information such as temperature, print head positions and extrusion rates. Only the sliced GCODE file can be loaded by the printer.

Slicing: from model to print

Imagine you want to bake a gorgeous loaf of bread. What's the best way to do it? Right, you mix and knead all the ingredients. In 3D printing, you mix your ingredients in a CAD program, and the bread is digitally in front of you. You can see it on the screen. Now you feel hungry.

To print the bread, you need to help your printer cut the digital bread into slices so that the printer can now produce the bread slice by slice in reality. It would be best if you "sliced" the bread.

The slicing process is crucial to the success of the print. The 3D model is broken down into layers and translated into G-code. The choice of slicer - whether Cura, PrusaSlicer, OrcaSlicer or Simplify3D - significantly impacts the result. These software packages offer a variety of settings to optimise print quality, including layer height, infill patterns and support structures. Try them all out. The result is always a GCode. But each programme has its peculiarities, design, strengths and weaknesses. Many printer manufacturers supply a variant of the above software as a licence, and as every user has their preferences, you will like one program better than another. Some programs offer much better support, while others are easier to use.

Be open and accept failure during the learning curve. Most programs are offered free of charge by the manufacturer and are usually open to third-party extensions to a certain extent.

 Tip: Find YOUR slicer. I started with Cura back then, not because it seemed easy to me, but because Elegoo supplied its own version of Cura. The first print results were nice, and Cura has many add-ons that you can easily add to the programme. It's really great.

Then I got curious and tried Orca. Initially, I didn't find Orca very clearly, so I went back to Cura. However, I realised that I could only solve various challenges with Orca. So I switched to Orca. Today I use both slicers depending on the subject. I can now quickly recognise which slicer brings the motif onto the print bed best, fastest or cleanest. So the same applies here - try it out. Since I bought the Kobra 3 Combo, I even used the Bambulab slicer to understand how the designers have planned a motif. Of course, you can also print Bambulab designs on other printers.

File transfer

From computer to printer, there are several ways to transfer the G-code file to the 3D printer:

SD card/USB stick: The traditional method involves copying the G-code to an SD card or USB stick and then inserting it into the printer. This method is reliable and straightforward but requires manually transferring the file from the computer to the printer.

Manufacturer App: Some Manufacturers (e.g., Anycubic) offer you complete control and observation of your 3D Printer with their own App on your mobile device. This offers quick and reliable access to your printer, but most of the time, it also limits the printer to only the manufacturer's app, and any access via Fluidd (see below) is no longer possible.

Network transfer: Many modern 3D printers can transfer files directly over the home network. This can be done via Wi-Fi or Ethernet, enabling seamless printer integration into your digital working environment. Programmes such as OctoPrint extend this functionality by allowing remote control and monitoring of the printing process. In most cases, connecting the printer to your router is sufficient using an existing RJ45 connection. After some time, your printer should have received an IP address from the router. Enter this in the web browser, and if your printer is running under Klipper, you will see either the Fluidd or Mainsail front end.

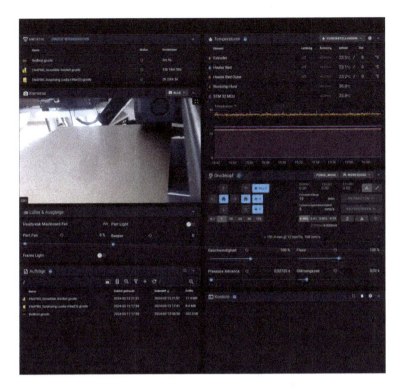

Figure 44 Fluidd Screenshot

Outlook

The importance of firmware A critical aspect that significantly affects the performance and capabilities of your printer is the firmware - the subject of our next chapter. The firmware controls every movement of the printer and every temperature change; it is the operating system of your 3D printer. In the next chapter, we'll look at the differences and benefits of Marlin and Klipper, two leading firmware options, and how they affect print quality, speed and ease of use. Printing a model of the iconic British time-travelling cabin is a shining example of the creative and limitless world of 3D printing.

The famous Time Travel series and 3D printing analogy reflect impressive technological development. As the Time Travel series character teaches us, the real magic lies not in escaping reality but in bravely confronting the unknown, equipped with curiosity and the determination to make the impossible a reality. 3D printing is our time-travelling vehicle, an instrument that gives us the power to navigate through the dimensions of creativity and shape the future in the present - and it always seems bigger from the inside than from the outside.

Firmware options and their impact on 3D printing

In the complex world of 3D printing, the firmware, the heart of every 3D printer, plays a crucial role. It controls the fine movements and thermal management and is the interface through which our designs are turned into reality. As you may have read in the last chapters, I modified my printers to upgrade their performance, enhance their printing quality, or simply get a better overview of my prints.

This chapter takes you on a journey of discovery through the famous Marlin and Klipper firmware options. It highlights the innovative integration with OctoPrint, a tool that extends the capabilities of your 3D printer. Which firmware is correct for you? The choice of firmware affects essential printer functions such as motion control, temperature management and user interaction. Marlin is known for its reliability and broad compatibility and provides a solid platform for many printer owners. It is characterised by a high level of customizability, which makes it attractive to both beginners and experienced users. Marlin is mainly used for low-cost entry-level models, as the hardware requirements for the MCU (no, not Marvel's) and the microcontroller unit are not that high.

This contrasts with Klipper, a firmware that utilises a distributed processing architecture. By offloading computationally intensive tasks to a more powerful computer, such as a Raspberry Pi, Klipper enables impressive improvements in speed and accuracy. This approach requires deeper technical understanding and careful configuration but rewards users with performance that often exceeds that of traditional firmware options.

Figure 45 Raspberry 3b

An exciting chapter in the world of 3D printing is the ability to update or modify the firmware of devices to unlock new features or improve performance. Such a switch from Marlin to Klipper, supported by the computing power of a Raspberry Pi, is an excellent example of the flexibility and adaptability of modern 3D printers. For example, a printer powered initially by Marlin can rise to new heights with the advanced features and increased efficiency of Klipper.

Tip: Sometimes, the effort to convert a printer from Marlin to Klipper is too significant or impossible because the network resources are unavailable. In such a case, I tuned my printer (e.g. Creality Ender3) to Octoprint (https://octoprint.org). It feels like Klipper and offers a variety of add-ons. It is a fan project of a German programmer (Gina Häußge) who keeps this project alive through donations. The community then diligently develops the add-ons, which they also offer for free. Of course, free does not mean that you cannot support the project. Remember, this project may help your printer perform better and save you money for a new printer.

Figure 46 Octoprint Logo

Another Brick in the Wall?

However, caution is advised. A humorous but severe warning: not every firmware update goes smoothly. There have been cases where printers have been left in a "bricked" state - literally as useful as a brick - after a failed flash update. This emphasises how important it is to prepare carefully for the flash process and to be aware that while the chances of success are high, the risk of failure can never be eliminated.

Figure 47 Bricked Mainboard of a 3D Printer – looks nice, does nothing.

Github, Discord and Co.

Fortunately, the community around 3D printing, especially firmware such as Klipper and Marlin, is constructive and full of resources. Platforms such as GitHub, Discord, and YouTube have numerous guides and tutorials that detail the process of changing firmware. These resources are invaluable, not only for successfully flashing the firmware but also for understanding the deeper workings of your 3D printer. They provide step-by-step instructions, best practices and sometimes even specific solutions to common problems when updating the firmware.

 Klipper's Discord server can be found here: https://discord.klipper3d.org

In general, you can discover Discord servers on 3D printing at this link: https://disboard.org/de/servers/tag/3d-printing

Figure 48 GitHub Logo

The famous scene from a well-known travel guide to outer space, where our protagonist realises that his house is being demolished, reminds us of the possible consequences of a failed firmware update with a humorous sideways glance at our topic. Just as the novel character was surprised, you might be surprised if you flash the firmware unprepared and your printer suddenly stops working. But as the book says, don't panic! The community and its resources are ready to help and ensure your printer becomes something other than another build on a space bypass.

SLA Printing

A Brief In-Depth Look 3D printing has revolutionised the manufacturing landscape, and in this broad field, stereolithography (SLA) occupies a special place. This chapter aims to take a wider look at SLA, from its historical roots to its technical intricacies to its applications and challenges. The development of SLA printing technology began in the 1980s when Chuck Hull, often referred to as the father of 3D printing, invented and patented the first working SLA printing system. This groundbreaking invention laid the foundation for additive manufacturing by enabling the layer-by-layer construction of objects from liquid resin. Since then, SLA technology has continued to evolve, with improvements in speed, precision and the variety of materials that can be used. Detailed description of the process At the heart of SLA printing is the UV laser, which is guided precisely over the surface of the liquid resin to cure the material layer by layer. At a molecular level, the UV radiation causes polymerisation, in which the monomeric and oligomeric resin components cross-link to form solid polymer chains. This chemical reaction is the secret behind the ability of SLA printing to produce highly detailed and structurally complex objects.

Photopolymer resins are at the heart of SLA printing and are available in various formulations, each with specific properties that make them suitable for different applications. Standard resins offer a good balance between strength and flexibility , and speciality resins are ideal for applications that require high temperatures, flexibility, or biocompatibility. Choosing the suitable resin is crucial to achieving the desired results.

Comparison with other 3D printing technologies

Although SLA is known for its precision and surface quality, each 3D printing technology offers unique advantages. For example, FDM printers are cheaper and easier to use, while SLS (Selective Laser Sintering) enables the production of parts without support structures. A comparison of these technologies shows that the choice of the appropriate process depends heavily on the specific project requirements. Application examples and case studies SLA printing is used in many fields, from medicine to art. One outstanding example is the use of SLA in dentistry, where customised crowns and bridges can be produced with unprecedented precision. Such case studies demonstrate the versatility and potential of SLA technology.

Future developments and research

SLA printing technology is not standing still. Current research is focused on developing new resin formulations that enable faster printing and improving UV light sources for even more precise curing. These advances promise to push the boundaries of what is possible.

Safety precautions and environmental aspects

Safety precautions are essential when handling photopolymer resins, as many resins are toxic. Wearing protective equipment and disposing of waste properly are essential to minimise health risks. At the same time, the industry is researching more environmentally friendly resin alternatives to reduce the environmental footprint of SLA printing.

In the exciting world of stereolithography printing, at the intersection where today's technology and the sci-fi visions of yesteryear merge, the use of photopolymer resins reminds us of the wise lessons of a legendary space series. Like the fearless crew of a lunar station confronted with unknown and often dangerous substances in the vastness of space, we, too, must exercise the utmost caution and prudence when using these resins.

This series, famous for its realistic portrayal of life and challenges in a harsh and unexplored space environment, reminds us to be careful when handling materials that pose potential health risks. Just like the brave space explorers who found unconventional solutions to the challenges of the cosmos, the process of SLA printing urges us to act responsibly and take preventative measures to minimise any hazards.

Special printing forms

Multi-colour printing with one or more extruders

Multifilament printers, such as those from BambuLab or Anycubic, can print with several filaments simultaneously on one extruder, thus producing multi-coloured or multi-material objects in a single printing process.

The advantages of this technology are considerable. However, multifilament printers also place higher demands on the user: the correct setting and calibration of the machine can be complex, and using different coloured filaments leads to higher consumption. If you have just printed with black and now want to switch to yellow, you first have to push the filament out of the extruder and nozzle somewhere before you can continue printing with yellow. If you want to return to black, the whole process starts again.

The printers dispose of the wrong filament in the motif, a cleaning tower or by placing it to one side in a container. In addition, these printers are often a bit more expensive to purchase and operate, and the printing process can take longer due to the added complexity.

Despite these challenges, multifilament printers are opening up new horizons in 3D printing by pushing the boundaries of what is possible. The market is still relatively young. In the meantime, more and more start-ups on Kickstarter are entering the market with multifilament printers.

If you have been working with a computer for a while, the terms CGA, EGA, VGA and Bernstein may still ring a bell. Today, it is taken for granted that your computer and monitor can display all spectrum colours without delay. That used to be different.

Development has yet to stand still - it is foreseeable that in 5-10 years' time, monochrome consumer filament printers will hardly be found on the market. The textile embroidery industry is currently undergoing a similar process. Google for Coloreel, and you will be amazed.

Another idea for multi-colour printing is to use a multi-filament extruder. Now that you know how your extruder works, use several of them in your printer. Many hobbyists convert their printers themselves. Adapting the software to the offset between the several extruders is another challenge.

Multicolour printing with a mono-colour printer

But now you've just bought a single-extruder, single-colour 3D printer and now we're saying that the market for these models is ending. Well, it's not that bad, and to a certain extent, you can also print multicolour with your printer.

The Makro M600 helps us with that. Marlin already programmed it on delivery, but some Klipper printers still have to learn it. Anyway, in any slicer, you can send an M600 (read above for Macros) command to the printer at one (or more) layer height during slicing. The slicer software shows you the way.

M600 causes the printer to move the print head to the side BEFORE the layer begins, retract the filament and wait for you to insert the new filament into the extruder and extrude it until it comes out of the nozzle. Then you press "Continue" (usually a pause symbol) and the printer starts printing a new layer with the new colour. This way you can actually print in multiple colours. Of course, 5 colour changes take a lot of time.

Lithopanes

Lithophanes (or lithophanes) are unique 3D-printed products that are a remarkable combination of art and engineering. Originally made from porcelain in the 19th century, they have been modernised through 3D printing. When lithophanes are 3D printed, an image is transformed into a thin, translucent sheet that reveals impressive shading and depth when backlit. The thickness of the material in different areas corresponds to the greyscale of the image: thinner areas let more light through and appear lighter, while thicker areas let less light through and appear darker. 3D printing has made the creation of lithophanes more accessible, as users can transform their own photos into these three-dimensional works of art. Specialised software cuts the image into different layers, which are then printed layer by layer, usually in white or slightly translucent filament such as PLA, to achieve the best results. The ability to customise the lithophane's size, thickness and even the curvature makes it a popular personalised gift or decorative item. Precision is crucial when printing lithophanes, as the most minor deviations in layer height or filament flow

 can affect the final image. The correct print speed and temperature setting is also crucial to ensure uniform translucency and detail. https://tool.itslitho.com/ lets you easily create an STL file from a JPG. You load this into your slicer and generate a Gcode from it.

Figure 49Printed Lithopane

Figure 50 Same Lithopane with Lights behind

Conclusion

The universe of 3D printing is as limitless as the human quest for creativity and innovation. The possibilities of this rapidly developing technology are almost unlimited. Yet, as comprehensive as it may be, our book can only cover a section of this vast and ever-changing field. The world of 3D printing is growing and changing at such a speed that it is almost impossible to capture every detail, every technology, and every new advance. But these infinite possibilities and constant evolution make 3D printing fascinating and rewarding.

Our primary goal in creating this book was to provide a comprehensive yet easy-to-understand introduction to 3D printing. We hope it will serve as a guide that will not only provide you with the technical know-how, but also give you the inspiration and confidence to embark on your own 3D printing adventure. However, the key to a successful entry into the world of 3D printing is not just reading this or any other book, but requires preparation, a thirst for knowledge and a willingness to keep learning.

The 3D printing community is an inexhaustible source of knowledge, support and inspiration. Platforms such as Discord servers and Facebook beginner groups not only offer instructions and answers to your questions but also a community that shares your passion for 3D printing. YouTube channels offer visual tutorials ranging from basic concepts to advanced techniques and problem-solving. These resources are essential as they provide knowledge, encouragement, and sense of community that is so important when venturing into new areas.

It is essential to remember that 3D printing is, first and foremost, a hobby - a passion that should bring joy and challenge and serve as a creative outlet. The journey through the world of 3D printing is a personal discovery characterised by a sense of achievement and learning moments. Every failed print, every solved problem and every successfully realised project contributes to your development as a 3D printing enthusiast.

You may encounter challenges that require patience and perseverance, but these challenges make the experience so rewarding. The satisfaction of creating a physical object that previously existed only as a digital idea is unrivalled. As you expand your skills and deepen your knowledge, you will realise that 3D printing is not just a hobby but also a constant source of inspiration and creativity.

In conclusion, we encourage you to plunge into the world of 3D printing. Stay calm by the wealth of information, but see it for what it is: tools in your hands waiting to be used creatively. 3D printing is a journey that begins with every print. It is a journey enriched by community, sharing experiences, and growing together. We invite you to become part of this ever-growing community, nurture your curiosity, be creative, and, above all, have fun with the process.

Welcome to the fascinating world of 3D printing, and have fun doing it.

Discover More: Beyond the First Layer

Congratulations! By reading this book, you've already mastered the critical "first layer" in 3D printing. But why stop there? On my upcoming YouTube channel, Beyond the First Layer, we dive deeper into the fascinating world of 3D printing, offering hands-on guidance tailored for beginners and those with a few hours of printing experience.

This isn't about flashy influencer gimmicks. It's a practical space where I share tutorials, product recommendations, and simple tips and tricks to complement what you've learned in this book. The goal? To help you take your 3D printing journey to the next level, one layer at a time.

While this book is a one-way street where I share my insights with you, YouTube opens up a two-way conversation. It's designed to be a vibrant forum for exchanging ideas, troubleshooting problems, and celebrating successes as a community.

 So, join me on Beyond the First Layer—follow the channel, subscribe, and explore what lies beyond the first layer!

https://www.youtube.com/@LayerGuru

About the author

Michael Hau, born in 1970, is not only a family man - married, father of a son, father-in-law and proud grandfather of a granddaughter - but also a passionate technology enthusiast whose passion for everything that lights up, beeps and moves with electricity goes back to his childhood. His fascination was awakened by the first broadcast of the TOS crew ("Star Trek"), a critical experience that had a decisive influence on his career.

Michael lives by the motto: "Technology must be compatible. Otherwise, we'll make it compatible." This maxim has guided him through countless technical challenges and innovations. He resisted buying a 3D printer for a long time, knowing that this would ignite a passion that could quickly get out of control. And that's precisely what happened. 3D printing is not just a hobby for him but a passion that fascinates and challenges him.

Michael enjoys attending conventions such as FedCon and immersing himself in the world that once laid the foundations for his technical dreams. He particularly appreciates that the "nerd" of the 70s, who was ridiculed back then, is now celebrated as a cool geek. For him, this social recognition is a sign of change that shows how far the enthusiasm for technology and innovation has come.

General note

The works mentioned in this book and their characters, concepts or scenarios are cited with due respect to the rights holders and for criticism, comment, reporting or teaching that might be considered fair use. These quotations express recognition and appreciation of the original works and their creators. They are used without commercial intent to promote cultural understanding and education.

Legal Disclaimer

The content of this book, including all written information, illustrations, and guidance, is the result of meticulous research and the author's personal experience. While every effort has been made to ensure accuracy and reliability, it is important to note that materials, devices, and technologies in 3D printing can vary significantly between manufacturers, models, and product generations.

Readers are advised to use the information provided in this book with caution and to verify its applicability to their specific circumstances, equipment, and materials. The author explicitly disclaims any responsibility or liability for damages, losses, or injuries resulting from applying or misusing the techniques, instructions, or recommendations described herein.

By using this book, you acknowledge and accept that all actions undertaken based on its content are at your own risk. The author neither guarantees specific outcomes nor assumes liability for any errors, omissions, or changes in technology that may render the information outdated or unsuitable. It is recommended to consult the respective manufacturer's guidelines and instructions when working with 3D printing materials or devices.

www.ingramcontent.com/pod-product-compliance
Lightning Source LLC
LaVergne TN
LVHW051643050326
832903LV00022B/863